Los Angeles Daily News

LEGACY

THE LOS ANGELES LAKERS'
UNFORGETTABLE RUN TO THE 2020 NBA TITLE

This book is available in quantity at special discounts for your group or organization.
For further information, contact:

Triumph Books LLC
814 North Franklin Street
Chicago, Illinois 60610
Phone: (312) 337-0747
www.triumphbooks.com

Printed in U.S.A.
ISBN: 978-1-62937-826-8

Southern California News Group
Ron Hasse, President & Publisher
Bill Van Laningham, Vice President, Marketing
Frank Pine, Executive Editor
Tom Moore, Executive Sports Editor
Michele Cardon and Dean Musgrove, Photo Editors

Content packaged by Mojo Media, Inc.
Joe Funk: Editor
Jason Hinman: Creative Director

Front and back cover photos by AP Images

CONTENTS

INTRODUCTION

By Kyle Goon

Before satellites and television, there were just the seats and the people in them. There was the hardwood and the lines and the hoops, but in the background has always been the roar of the crowd, breathing life and color into the dramatic moments that have forged champions.

Until 2020.

What I'll remember as much from the Lakers' 2020 championship season are the moments of silence — when the artificial noise was peeled away, the utter isolation of the NBA bubble was clearly felt. In the very moment when LeBron James, Anthony Davis and the team that had played through a 355-day NBA season should have been showered with the adulation of a fan base, both pent-up and heartbroken from an exhausting year, they had only their families and each other to bask in their achievement.

No NBA team has ever worked harder for longer. The NBA bubble was a season unto itself, one that saw lesser competitors wilt and fall by the wayside. The Lakers were not themselves at its start, and no one looked quite as vulnerable as James, a 35-year-old who initially looked uncomfortable without the creature comforts of his family and adoring Staples Center crowd.

But in the end, the Lakers found a way to run to the front of the line and stay there — as they had all season with smothering and physical defense accompanying the highlight-reel fast break assault.

This team had fun: There was ample evidence of that on social media, between birthday parties in tuxedos and pizza parties in the bubble. It was a season that seemed to shed years off James in particular, who was able to find both a next gear of his game and an element of comfort surrounded by Davis, an eager pupil, and a host of veterans. On a roster with six former champions, many said the Lakers had the best chemistry of any group they'd ever been a part of.

That sense of community was tested early and often — in the most extreme fashion.

From the moment the season began the Lakers were trapped inside Chinese hotels amid diplomatic uncertainty that thwarted a pair of preseason games. They picked up from that tense overseas episode by rolling out early to the lead in the Western Conference, winning 14 straight road games in one stretch and priding themselves on the psychological edge they held over their opponents in their own buildings. It helped that everywhere they went carried a sea of their own fans, purple and gold faithful ready to see light after the longest stretch of darkness the franchise has ever known.

The Lakers had a long and tumultuous journey to the 17th championship in franchise history. But even while missing fans in the stands, the accomplishment was sweet in the end. (AP Images)

But where they found reasons to celebrate on the court, the season dealt them body blows off it. The news of the deaths of Kobe and Gianna Bryant — a father-and-daughter duo that represented not only the glorious history of the Lakers but a lot of promise as well — shattered the Lakers and basketball fans world-wide. It was a hole no win could fill: The roses draped on the chairs where they watched their last game at Staples Center is a scene that's hard to forget.

If there's one critique to make: The longest season in NBA history was not enjoyed enough. A pandemic kept the fans who had hurt and healed along with their team out of the building where the championship was won. The soul of basketball is the five players on the floor — but the audience, in many ways, is what brings it to life.

Screens will never quite capture what this team, or its fans, endured. Maybe words will. ∎

BLOW OUT

Lakers Wallop the Heat in Game 1 of the NBA Finals

By Kyle Goon

From the postgame podium on Wednesday night, LeBron James wiped any sense of joy or accomplishment from his stony expression.

The Lakers had played their 27th game in the NBA bubble, and besides the screens and banners and court that screamed "NBA Finals," very little appeared different. But inside, the 35-year-old said, it felt "amazing."

"Felt great," he said. "I've been preparing for this moment for quite a while."

The emotions were reserved for the court on Game 1 of the NBA Finals, where the Lakers romped against the Miami Heat in a lopsided 116-98 victory that puts them three wins away from a championship they've openly talked about since June.

The Heat clogged the paint with their zone, and the Lakers threw a 3-point barrage. When the Heat tried stepping out to meet them, James and Anthony Davis almost effortlessly zig-zagged through the middle for dunks and big finishes.

The Lakers were the better rebounders, the better shooters, the better shot-swatters, the better ballhawks — by far the better team.

In the end with 1:23 left and a 17-point lead in hand, James checked himself out, satisfied that his 25 points, 13 rebounds and nine assists was good enough for a 1-0 start to the series. Through the middle of the game, the Lakers had a 45-point swing that left Miami choking on their dust for the entire second half.

Davis led with 34 points in his Finals debut, wrecking Miami's fine-tuned cuts to the basket with the swarming of his limbs and throwing down eight of his 11 field goals in the paint. It was the third-highest scoring Finals debut for a Laker, behind Shaquille O'Neal and George Mikan, and tied with Elgin Baylor.

The 27-year-old admitted he got some goosebumps to hear himself in that company.

"What makes it even more sweeter is winning it," he said. "And so obviously that's a great honor, but I also want to be mentioned in categories with champions, so that's the next step."

Brutal events for Miami made that more likely: Bam Adebayo (left shoulder) and Goran Dragic (left foot) were both out by the end of the third quarter. Adebayo had a strain, but Dragic, the Heat's leading scorer for the first three rounds of the playoffs, tore his plantar fascia, an injury that will almost certainly lead to missing games and will make for a much tougher uphill climb for Miami — already an underdog.

In each of their three previous series, the Heat had won the first two games. Jimmy Butler led his banged-up group with 23 points on 8 for 13 shooting, rookie Tyler Herro struggled on defense, Duncan Robinson

Anthony Davis (3) and LeBron James started the NBA Finals with a bang, dominating the Heat to the tune of a 116-98 win. (AP Images)

didn't score a point in 27 minutes, and the Heat (the No. 2 deep shooting team on threes) was held under 32 percent.

"We talk about how damn near perfect that we have to play, and that was nowhere near it," said Butler.

The Heat gave the Lakers a flutter early on, when Butler and Jae Crowder helped lead a 13-0 run that put the Lakers in an early hole, prompting a timeout.

But when the Lakers swapped Davis in at center, the scales swung wildly in the other direction. From the 3:44 mark when Kentavious Caldwell-Pope made a 3-pointer to halftime, the Lakers outscored the Heat by 30.

It was a strong night for the supporting cast, which helped the Lakers start 13 for 20 from 3-point range. Caldwell-Pope, Danny Green and Alex Caruso combined for 34 points, and their spacing helped roll over the Miami zone for James and Davis to finish the job.

The game was again sparsely attended on the restrictive Disney campus, but luminaries logged in digitally, including Lakers legends O'Neal, Kareem Abdul-Jabbar, James Worthy and Robert Horry. Dwyane Wade, a close friend of James and synonymous with the Heat, checked in on the virtual wall as well.

Davis was more excited by an in-person guest: his father, who recently got out of a 10-day quarantine.

The Lakers led by as much as 32 but a late rally started by Kendrick Nunn made the game closer than they wished. Citing a Game 2 letdown in his 2011 Finals against Dallas (which he lost), James said he was "amped up" to see film of the game to learn from the Lakers' mistakes.

"We got so much more work to do," he said. "The job is not done, and we're not satisfied with winning one game. It's that simple." ∎

LeBron James glides through the lane during the second half of the commanding Game 1 win. James had 25 points, 13 rebounds and nine assists. (AP Images)

NBA FINALS GAME 2

OCTOBER 2, 2020 | LAKE BUENA VISTA, FLORIDA

LAKERS 124, HEAT 114

DYNAMIC DUO

LeBron, AD Too Strong for Depleted Heat, Lakers Take 2-0 Lead in NBA Finals

By Kyle Goon

The last time two Lakers scored 30 points in the same NBA Finals game, LeBron James would have been watching on TV, just like everyone else. It was 2002, in Game 3 of an eventual sweep against the then-New Jersey Nets, their overmatched opponent, when Shaquille O'Neal and Kobe Bryant scored a combined 71 points. James was a teenager, marveling at O'Neal's unmatched power and the cocky shot-making of a young Bryant, just a few years older than him.

History never truly repeats itself, but it often rhymes: James and Anthony Davis have pushed their own Lakers squad to a 2-0 lead in the Finals behind their dominance in a 124-114 win over the Miami Heat in Game 2 on Friday night. And James, whose 33 points was just one more than his teammate, was tickled to meet the most dominant Lakers duo in one small way in the record books.

"I can't even believe I'm up here talking about myself and AD with Kobe and Shaq," he said, smirking.

Still if the Lakers are to match that 2002 feat — a sweep — they have a lot of work to do. Down two of their key players, the Heat signaled that they won't soon quit. The Lakers needed a couple of good punches, including a pair of baskets by James in the last three minutes, to make sure they could hold on. James scored 10 of his points in that last frame against Miami, which drew them to an even 21-21 in the fourth.

James also finished with nine assists and nine rebounds, while Davis notched 14 rebounds. But even the superstars, who James noted Thursday "aren't jealous of each other," had at least one spat during a stretch as the Heat piled up 39 points in the third quarter to resuscitate their chances in what looked like a blowout.

Davis smiled sheepishly: "Did y'all see something?"

But the Lakers tinkered with their defense and got stops on a team playing without Bam Adebayo and Goran Dragic, two of the Heat's three leading scorers. While Jimmy Butler put in a strong effort with 25 points and 13 assists, Miami was just 7 for 15 in the fourth quarter. The Lakers did not turn the ball over once in the final period.

With a wing-heavy lineup and Davis in the middle, the Lakers managed to get enough buckets to clinch the win, with a dagger coming by Kentavious Caldwell-Pope hitting just his second 3-pointer of the night on 11 attempts. The Lakers shot just 34 percent from deep, a key element to softening the zone.

But the simple fact remains: James and Davis are too much talent for the Heat to handle. And by the end, Davis said, his tiff with James was forgotten.

"We both want to be great, we both want to dominate the game," he said. "We had some blown coverages on the defensive end. We kind of just had that moment, put it behind us and kept playing."

The Heat started Meyers Leonard and Tyler Herro and rigidly stuck to their zone defense in an effort to

Anthony Davis began the game on fire, hitting 14 of 15 shots and eventually finishing with 32 points and 14 rebounds. (AP Images)

junk up the Lakers' penetration to the rim. But after a shaky first quarter in Game 1, the Lakers had little trouble for much of the game, scoring 74 points in the middle two quarters with decisive passing.

While wearing the Black Mamba jerseys in Game 2 of the Western Conference Finals, Davis hit the last shot to beat Denver. Donning the same threads in the Finals, Davis hit nearly all of his shots in the first three quarters, starting the game 14 for 15.

Matched up again with the Heat zone, Davis showed his nose for the rim early as the Lakers skip-passed around and through the defense, and Davis found ways to finish. In the third quarter, he added midrange shots from the right baseline, causing the Heat defenders to slump their shoulders in frustration.

"He's just so versatile," said Lakers guard Rajon Rondo who had 16 points and 10 assists. "He's damn near playing like the best player in the game. Hands down. I'm very fortunate he's on our team this year."

But Miami seemed impassioned by a stirring timeout speech from 40-year-old veteran Udonis Haslem in the third quarter, and they stemmed the tide after the Lakers went up by as much as 18 points and gradually began closing in. It didn't help the Lakers that their top two shooters slumped: Danny Green and Caldwell-Pope combined for 3 for 19 from 3-point range.

It was the first "bubble" game attended by Lakers owner Jeanie Buss, who jumped up and down and waved through the plexiglass barrier of the bubble's outer tier when she saw general manager Rob Pelinka down below shortly before tip-off. Klutch CEO Rich Paul was in another box, peering down at six of his clients on the Lakers roster.

Davis said the dark background to the court made it tough to see the audience.

The Lakers will continue to lean on each other to finish it out.

"We know we can be a lot better and we're just, myself and AD, we're not satisfied with just the win," James said. "We want to be great. We want to be great, as close to 48 minutes as possible." ∎

LeBron James one-upped teammate Anthony Davis with 33 points and added nine rebounds and nine assists. (AP Images)

NBA FINALS GAME 3

OCTOBER 4, 2020 | LAKE BUENA VISTA, FLORIDA

HEAT 115, LAKERS 104

TROUBLE BREWING

Jimmy Butler, Heat Punch Back in Game 3 to Stun Lakers

By Kyle Goon

After backing down Kentavious Caldwell-Pope and nailing a turnaround jumper in the fourth quarter, Jimmy Butler skipped back and lowered his hand three feet off the ground, as if patting a child on the head.

The message: Too small.

It applied to the Lakers, too, who shrunk the moment of Game 3 and could not match the desperation of their undermanned, outgunned opponent — or the Miami Heat's lone remaining All-Star Butler, who turned in the night of his life with 40 points, 11 rebounds and 13 assists to outpace both LeBron James and Anthony Davis in a 115-104 Miami win. The Lakers lead the series 2-1 with Game 4 coming Tuesday.

It was a vexing evening for Los Angeles, which could not seem to find a rhythm. James had 25 points and Davis had 15, and both were frustrated for much of the night all the way down to the final seconds, losing the chance to take a commanding lead and be one game away from a title. It was a game of slumped shoulders, of pounding the ball into the court after Heat baskets, of Lakers appearing to bicker after blown assignments.

The Lakers could not leave soon enough. After a shot clock violation, there was 0.7 seconds remaining in the game and the Lakers had the ball, but James had exited the AdventHealth Arena court, leaving Jared Dudley to sub in on his behalf.

When asked if his early departure was frustration or thinking the game was over, James had a terse one-word response: "Both."

Butler had the kind of performance James is known for. He's one of just three men to score 40 points with a triple double in the Finals: Jerry West and James himself. According to Elias Sports Bureau, it was the only Finals game where James has been out-scored, out-rebounded and out-assisted in his 10 Finals appearances.

It wasn't the only part of James' game that Butler imitated. In the fourth quarter, cameras caught Butler telling James, "They're in trouble." He said afterward that James had said it to the Heat in the first quarter, when the Lakers looked to be recovering after a sluggish start. The two men have a history of competitive squawking, but so far James has a 10-4 record against Butler in the playoffs.

"I think LeBron has got the best of me way too many times," Butler said. "I respect the guy for it, but this is a different time now, a different group of guys that I have around me, and we are here to win, we are here to compete."

The Lakers did not look prepared, despite playing a second game without having to face injured starters Bam Adebayo and Goran Dragic. Even without two of their three leading scorers, the Heat still hurt the Lakers by shooting 63 percent inside the arc and racking up 52 points in the paint.

In particular, the Lakers had trouble tracking

shooting big Kelly Olynyk, who slipped screens and scored 17 points, getting the lion's share of Adebayo's missing minutes. It was the swarming, multi-faceted Miami the Lakers had been talking up for a week, but they still looked spun around by the Heat's never-ending swirl of actions and screens.

"We were getting confused on a lot of things," Davis said. "They had wide open looks that they missed early and made late from three. We let Jimmy get into a strong hand too many times, getting to the basket, getting and-ones or getting to the free throw line. We were letting guys get to the rim easily with no contact."

It had been some time since a passive start by Davis, and of the playoff run, it was one of his least productive. Davis turned the ball over four times in the first quarter before even attempting a shot. With some adjustments to the Heat's zone, Davis looked uncomfortable and had trouble connecting with James on entry passes. In the second quarter just as he started gaining some rhythm with a 3-pointer and alley-oop, he was sidelined for the last five minutes of the half after his third foul.

The Lakers made do with unconventional lineups, including throwing in J.R. Smith for just his 10th playoff appearance. The 35-year-old shouted "Still got it!" after hitting his first 3-pointer of the Finals in the second quarter, off an assist from his longtime teammate James.

The Lakers reached a low point in the third quarter when the out-of-sync starting lineup surrendered an 8-0 Heat run, putting them in a 14-point hole. But instead of making substitutions, Vogel allowed the group to play through it, and by the end of the third, the margin was five.

A Rajon Rondo layup over Duncan Robinson put the Lakers up 91-89 in the fourth quarter. But the Heat didn't allow it to become a turning point, taking the lead back a minute later on an Olynyk 3-pointer.

The Lakers bench was an enormous part of the effort, as both Markieff Morris and Kyle Kuzma scored 19 points. But it underscored how little the Lakers got from the rest of their starters, particularly Danny Green and Kentavious Caldwell-Pope who had a second straight disappointing shooting night (1 for 11). Davis' 15 points was his second-lowest scoring night of the playoffs.

James was the only starter who scored a field goal in the fourth quarter.

Even though Lakers were frustrated in the loss and to extend their stay in the NBA bubble to at least Friday night, they spoke confidently about their ability to bounce back. The Lakers have yet to lose consecutive games in these playoffs, and even though James as much as anyone respects Miami's resilience — from Pat Riley on down the line — he also has faith in the team he has.

"We're not concerned: We know we can play a lot better," he said. "We have another opportunity to take a commanding lead on Tuesday. You relish that opportunity." ∎

NBA FINALS GAME 4

OCTOBER 6, 2020 | LAKE BUENA VISTA, FLORIDA

LAKERS 102, HEAT 96

RISING TO THE CHALLENGE

Lakers Gut Out Victory Over Heat in Game 4, Now One Win Away from Championship

By Kyle Goon

The Miami Heat announced two days before that the NBA Finals would be no coronation: The Lakers would have to earn everything they got.

And earn it they did: Tuesday night's Game 4 was an exercise in sweat and hustle, requiring every ounce of attention and will the Lakers had. And now they're just one more victory from a title.

The end looked familiar, a 102-96 win that saw the Lakers go up 3-1 in the series. Anthony Davis beat his chest after a 3-pointer that put them ahead by nine with 39.5 seconds left, and he and LeBron James screamed and beat their chests letting out all the steam that had built up after two days of swallowing their first loss of the series.

James scored 28, Davis scored 22, and the Lakers kept up an impressive streak: In this postseason, they have never lost back-to-back games.

Still, even by their own standards, this one loomed particularly large. James sent a group text Tuesday morning to the team that he had never sent before in the bubble: He called Game 4 "a must-win."

"I felt like for me personally, this was one of the biggest games of my career," he said. "And I wanted to relay that message to my teammates, what type of zone I was in."

The final three minutes clinched it, a 10-5 run that saw the Lakers lean on more than just their stars. Kentavious Caldwell-Pope (15 points) started the rally with a corner 3-pointer, spacing out quickly after a Heat turnover. In the next possession, he drove to the right of an overwhelmed Duncan Robinson, finishing off the glass.

Rajon Rondo's only points of the game came with 1:25 left — a finger-roll layup moments after a hard on-court collision with James going after a rebound. After six misses to start the game, it was a needed cap for a seven-rebound, five-assist night.

But it was Davis who again came up with the big shot, not far from where he nailed his game-winner against Denver in the Western Conference Finals. The 27-year-old had been hunting confidence since a meek Game 3 in which he scored just 15 points. Seeing the aggressive side come out at just the right moment lifted his teammates.

Said Caldwell-Pope: "AD is a game-changer when he's knocking down shots like that."

After two games of the Lakers' steady dominance followed by a Game 3 uppercut from the Heat, Game

Anthony Davis (3) pulls a rebound away from Miami's Bam Adebayo (13) and Kelly Olynyk (9) during the second half of the crucial Game 4 win. Davis stuffed the stat sheet with 22 points, nine rebounds, four assists and four blocks. (AP Images)

4 had a gritty feel of a series settling into the trenches with lots of shoves and tumbles to the court. Davis was scratched over his right eye in the fourth quarter, while Alex Caruso was hip-checked to the ground in the second.

Arguably the biggest adjustment by the Lakers was to set Davis on the Heat's Jimmy Butler, his long arms corralling a good deal of the killer cuts the All-Star guard had in a high-scoring triple-double Sunday. By the second half, James too was ready to play long minutes and stopped switching off of Butler on the defensive end.

After hitting his first five shots, Butler was held to just 3 for 12 for the rest of the game. He had 20 points, just half of his Game 3 output.

"That was a big part of our plan, the adjustments from last game to this game was to try to keep those guys on (Butler) as much as possible," Vogel said. "They rose to the challenge. They really stepped up."

The Lakers also made a second-half adjustment of going small, starting Markieff Morris over Dwight Howard to better keep up with the return of Bam Adebayo.

James' promise to be better on his turnovers was unrealized in the first a half: He coughed up five giveaways in an unsteady first half that mirrored his Game 3 performance. He and Davis seemed off on post-up entry passes, leading to the squabbles that also plagued them on that upending Sunday night.

At halftime, both James and Davis had just eight points apiece with a two-point lead.

But the third quarter saw both men pick up. James got going with a pair of 3-pointers early, while Davis hit shots later in the period. By the fourth, both had 17 points.

The motivation for the game was being outworked by the Heat two nights before. Davis said a film study of Game 3 set a fire within the locker room that they didn't want it to happen again.

"If we play like that every game — especially next game," Davis said, "then we become champions." ■

Kentavious Caldwell-Pope attacks the basket while Jae Crowder defends during the Game 4 win. Caldwell-Pope made his presence felt in the game with 15 points and five assists, as well as hitting multiple big shots late in the contest. (AP Images)

NBA FINALS GAME 5

OCTOBER 9, 2020 | LAKE BUENA VISTA, FLORIDA

HEAT 111, LAKERS 108

DENIED

Lakers Miss Chance to Clinch, as Heat Extend NBA Finals

By Mirjam Swanson

LeBron James put his head down, put the Lakers on his back and almost lifted them over the finish line and onto the mountaintop where the franchise's NBA-record-tying 17th championship awaits.

But Jimmy Butler is capable of some heavy lifting too.

Miami's leading man had 35 points, 12 rebounds and 11 assists, notching his second triple-double of these NBA Finals as he and his scrappy Heat squad fended off elimination Friday, beating the Lakers 111-108 and denying them history, at least for a night.

"Throughout the highs, throughout the lows, you stay even-keeled and get better with the process," said James, focused and matter of fact following the loss. "We gotta be better in Game 6 … and close the series."

The 35-year-old James turned in a stellar 40-point, 13-rebound, seven-assist performance and went back and forth with Butler down the stretch at AdventHealth Arena in Lake Buena Vista, Fla., where the NBA bubble will remain intact for at least two more days.

In the final minutes Friday, the two leading men took turns scoring a combined 13 points, on an array of jumpers and drives and free throws. The lead changed hands six times in the final two minutes, the most in a Finals game in 25 years, according to Elias Sports Bureau.

"That's the beauty of the game, being able to compete at the highest level," James said. "You take

those opportunities and you live in the moment. You're trying to make plays for your team and be successful on both ends, and we were both just trying to do that and trying to will our team to a victory.

"He was able to make one more play than I was able to make tonight and come away with a victory."

The Heat finally got the ball out of James' hands and into Kentavious Caldwell-Pope's, who missed a shot with 23.9 seconds left — but James' co-star Anthony Davis was there to clean up.

Davis — who was hobbled by a heel injury and still contributed 28 points, 12 rebounds, three blocked shots and three steals — was there for the offensive rebound and the putback to give the Lakers a 108-107 lead with just 21.8 seconds left between them and the franchise's first championship in a decade.

But Butler wasn't done. Driving again and drawing a foul on Davis — one of two down the stretch that the Lakers took issue with — Butler made both foul shots and again Miami led, 109-108 with 16.8 seconds to go.

"I left it all out there on the floor along with my guys, and that's how we're going to have to play from here on out," said Butler, who added five steals. "It's win or win for us. But this is the position that we're in. We like it this way."

James drove into the teeth of the Miami defense and delivered a pass to Danny Green, stationed wide open at the top of the arc. But Green — who, with James, can become one of only four players to have won NBA titles with a trio of teams — clanged an open 3-pointer off the front of the rim.

"It's one of the best shots that we could have got, I feel, in that fourth quarter, especially down the stretch with two guys on me, Duncan Robinson and Jimmy, and Danny had a hell of a look," James said. "It just didn't go down."

Markieff Morris corralled the long rebound but threw it away on an attempted lob pass to Davis and Miami had the ball back with 2.2 seconds left.

The Lakers — who were out of timeouts — fouled Tyler Herro to stop the clock, and the rookie made both free throws to extend the lead to 111-108.

"It was a good game, trading baskets," Davis said. "Just needed one stop."

Friday's defeat is the first blemish on James' previously perfect personal closeout record; he now is 3-1 in closeout opportunities in the Finals. And this season's Lakers now fall to 3-1 in closeout games in the bubble.

They also lost for the first time in the bubble in their Black Mamba jerseys, uniforms designed by Kobe Bryant and brought out for these playoffs, in which the Lakers now are 4-1.

"We wanted to come out and win the game, especially wearing those jerseys," Davis said. "But you come back, you look at the film, fix your mistakes and then come out in Game 6 remembering how close we were. If we don't make our mistakes, we win the game. So you kind of use it as fuel, but we're still up in the series. We win one; they have to win two. We have to keep that in mind."

"We'll definitely bounce back, there's no question about that," Lakers coach Frank Vogel said. "It's a tough loss, there's no doubt about it, we were very close … but our group's fine. We're gonna bounce back strong."

There were 16 lead changes and seven ties in all Friday, as the game went back and forth until its conclusion.

Duncan Robison added 26 points for Miami, for which six of seven players who saw the floor scored in double figures. Only veteran Andre Iguodala was scoreless, though he contributed timely defense and rebounding.

The Lakers got a fright late in the first quarter when Davis banged his heel while jockeying for a rebound. The seven-time All-Star reached down and grabbed his right heel, limped off the court and then lay down behind the baseline, where he was tended to by trainers.

Davis — who was leading the Lakers early with eight points, three rebounds, a steal and a blocked shot at the time — never went back to the locker room, however, and spent the quarter break pacing on the sideline, ready to return despite aggravating a right heel contusion he suffered initially in the Western Conference finals.

"It kind of just wore off and got back to normal," Davis said. "Just kept moving around, trying not to sit down, keep the adrenaline going and I was able to keep going, keep playing." ■

NBA FINALS GAME 6

OCTOBER 11, 2020 | LAKE BUENA VISTA, FLORIDA

LAKERS 106, HEAT 93

JOB'S FINISHED!

Lakers Win 17th NBA Title with Dominant Game 6 Effort

By Mirjam Swanson

Now LeBron James will be hailed as Lakers royalty.

"What I've learned being a Laker," James said as he and his teammates closed in on the franchise's 17th NBA title and his fourth, "is that the Laker faithful don't give a damn what you've done before."

Forevermore, those fans will be indebted to King James.

And to A.D., to Playoff Rondo, AC Fresh and KCP …

Together on Sunday, on their 95th day in the enclosed campus at Walt Disney World Resort, the Lakers put an exclamation point on the league's longest season with a 106-93 bubble-bursting championship blowout of the Miami Heat in Game 6 of the NBA Finals.

"You have written your own inspiring chapter in the great Laker history," Lakers controlling owner Jeanie Buss told the team moments after the victory that pulled the franchise even with the Boston Celtics for the most NBA championships in league history. It's the Lakers' first title since 2010, when five-time champ Kobe Bryant and crew outlasted the Celtics in seven games.

"It means a lot to represent this franchise," James said. "I told Jeanie when I came here, I was gonna put this franchise back in a position where it belongs."

In his second season in L.A., James partnered with Anthony Davis to guide a Lakers team that hadn't made the playoffs in six seasons back to the top of the podium — capping a 16-5 playoff run with a no-doubt-about-it dismantling of a doggedly competitive Miami team.

On Friday, L.A. failed to capitalize on a closeout opportunity for the first time this postseason, but first-year Lakers coach Frank Vogel had his team ready to make up for it two days later as the Lakers "took out some pent-up aggression and frustration" on the Heat, as Alex Caruso put it.

James led Sunday's attentive attack, with a full-steam-ahead triple-double: a team-high 28 points and 10 assists to go with 14 rebounds.

The multi-talented 35-year-old was named Finals MVP, becoming the first player to earn the honor with three teams, having previously done it in 2012 and 2013 with the Heat and in 2016 with Cleveland.

And in his 260th playoff game, James surpassed former Laker Derek Fisher for most postseason contests played in NBA history. He also improved his personal Finals record to 4-6, as one of only four players to

Anthony Davis finishes strong in traffic during the first half of the Game 6 win. Davis dropped 19 points and 15 rebounds on the way to winning the first championship of his career. (AP Images)

appear in 10 or more NBA Finals series, along with Bill Russell, Sam Jones and Kareem Abdul-Jabbar.

"(When) I took the job, we didn't have Anthony Davis, we didn't have the whole team … but I have always believed in LeBron James," Vogel said. "He's the greatest player the basketball universe has ever seen, and if you think you know, you don't know, until you're around him every day, you're coaching him, you're seeing his mind, you're seeing his adjustments, seeing the way he leads the group."

Davis arrived via a blockbuster trade for Lonzo Ball, Brandon Ingram, Josh Hart and three first-round picks. Davis spent most of the season playing power forward, but with a championship at stake Sunday, he accepted an assignment to play center, and despite an injured heel, he confounded the Heat, finishing with 19 points and 15 rebounds to help secure his first championship.

Rajon Rondo exhibited the playoff brilliance he's become known for, with 19 points on 8-for-11 shooting, many of them on drives to the basket. It's the second title for the 14th-year point guard, who won his first in 2008, when his Boston Celtics defeated the Lakers.

In his first playoff start, Caruso brought his usual energy, contributed five assists and was a team-best plus-20 in the box score.

And Kentavious Caldwell-Pope — who was booed, remember, by Lakers fans early this season — came through again in a big moment, with 17 points and some stellar defense on the Heat's dangerous shooters.

Danny Green, hotly criticized for missing an open 3-pointer that could have delivered the title two days earlier, on Sunday finished with 11 points, including going for 3 for 7 from 3-point range. Along with James, Green becomes one of only four players to have won a championship with three franchises.

"We wanted to treat it like it was Game 7, and we wanted to come out in the first quarter and impose our will, which we wasn't doing to start the series," Caldwell-Pope said. "But tonight, we came out with a fire."

LeBron James explodes for the dunk, two of his 28 points to go along with 14 rebounds and 10 assists, clinching his fourth championship and fourth NBA Finals MVP. (AP Images)

These Lakers got started just about a calendar year ago with preseason dates in China, where the Lakers found themselves in the middle of an international controversy stemming from a tweet by Houston Rockets general manager Daryl Morey supporting Hong Kong's pro-democracy protests.

In January, Bryant was killed along with his daughter Gianna and seven others in a helicopter crash.

The coronavirus suspended play for more than four months and social justice issues weighed heavily on members of the NBA, which cultivated a plan to finish the season safely in a bubble in Lake Buena Vista, Fla., where Sunday, the Lakers were the last team standing.

"We have a PhD in adversity, I can tell you that much," Vogel said. "We've been through a lot. I'm so damn proud of this team."

There was no on-court adversity Sunday, when L.A. used determined defense and a 36-16 second-quarter lead to build a 64-36 halftime advantage, the second-largest in NBA Finals history.

Although Miami never stopped going through the motions, cutting what had a been a 36-point deficit to 21 when it got it to 90-69 with 8:37 remaining, the Lakers didn't waver, unwilling to extend their stay in the bubble one day longer.

"It was great to share this stage with them," Heat coach Erik Spoelstra said of the Lakers. "Congratulations on the championship. They earned it."

No one made them earn it like Jimmy Butler, the Heat forward who was averaging 29 points, 10.8 assists and 8.6 rebounds and who willed Miami past the Lakers twice this series. On Sunday, he was all but stymied, finishing with a more-mortal 12 points, seven rebounds and eight assists.

The gutsy Goran Dragic played for the first time since Game 1, when he suffered a torn plantar fascia in his left foot. But the Heat's veteran point guard wasn't his true self, scoring five points in 19 minutes. ■

Rajon Rondo, seen here with his son Rajon Jr, was one of many players who had family join the NBA bubble as the playoffs progressed. Rondo had several big moments throughout the postseason, including 19 points, four rebounds and four assists in the deciding Game 6. (AP Images)

FOR KOBE

Kobe Bryant in Lakers' Hearts, on Their Minds After Winning NBA Title

By Elliott Teaford

Now it's done. The torch has been passed again, handed from George Mikan to Jerry West and Wilt Chamberlain to Magic Johnson and Kareem Abdul-Jabbar to Kobe Bryant and Shaquille O'Neal to Bryant and Pau Gasol and now to LeBron James and Anthony Davis.

One must imagine Bryant proud, smiling and cheering.

The Lakers won their record-tying 17th NBA championship on Sunday night with a commanding 106-93 victory over the Miami Heat in the decisive Game 6 of the Finals, a win that was 10 years in the making, through toil and turmoil and through one unimaginable loss.

Bryant's tragic death in a helicopter crash in January shook Laker Nation, Southern California and the entire basketball world to its core. Their grief was everywhere, and it went on for days, weeks and months. You saw it in the flowers and balloons and notes left at Staples Center and L.A. Live.

You saw it in the murals that popped up here and there, street art with heavy hearts.

You saw it in the tears and you heard it in the impromptu chants.

"Ko-be, Ko-be, Ko-be."

The Lakers played on and on, through their heartache, through a coronavirus pandemic that halted play for 4-1/2 months, through a social justice movement that boiled over from coast to coast and

around the globe and into the NBA bubble in Orlando, Fla., after the death of George Floyd.

Bryant and his family were never far from the Lakers' hearts and minds. "One, two, three Mamba," they would chant, referring to his Black Mamba nickname, after putting their hands together before heading onto the court to start every game, every quarter, every half and after every timeout.

"We didn't let him down, we didn't let him down," center Anthony Davis said. "Ever since the tragedy, all we wanted to do was do it for him. We didn't let him down. It would have been great to do it last game in his jerseys. But it made us come out more aggressive, more powerful on both ends of the floor to make sure we closed it out (Sunday). I know he's looking down on us, proud of us. I know Vanessa (Bryant's wife) is proud of us, the organization is proud of us.

"It means a lot to us. He was a big brother to all of us. We did this for him."

Davis referred to the Black Mamba jerseys designed by Bryant before his death and worn by the Lakers during the season and during the playoffs, and of which James said before wearing them in a loss to the Heat in Game 5 on Friday, "It means something, something more than just a uniform."

The Lakers rolled through the Portland Trail Blazers, Houston Rockets, Denver Nuggets and then the Heat, ending the longest season in NBA history. The Lakers' first title in 10 years ignited celebrations around Southern California. Fireworks exploded in the skies.

Fans gathered at Staples Center, clogging the streets

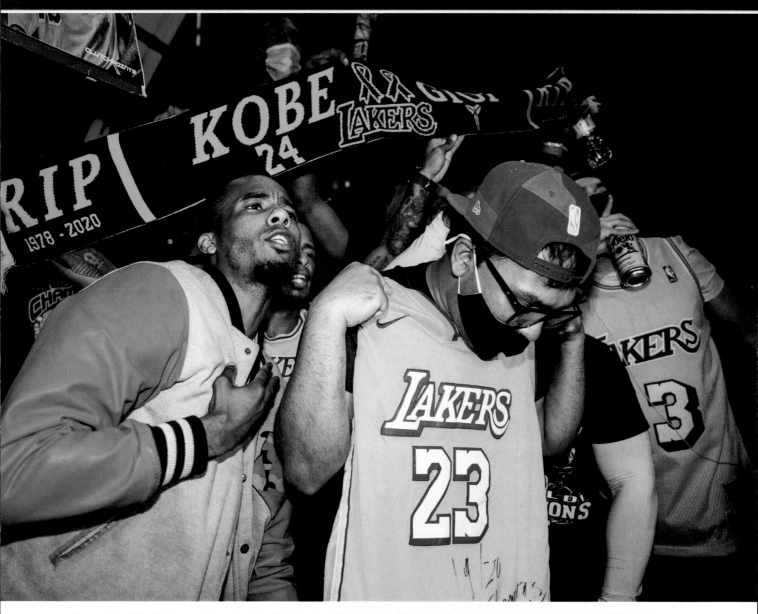

Fans outside of Staples Center celebrate both the 17th championship in franchise history and the legacy of the late, great Kobe Bryant. (AP Images)

despite officials' pleas to stay away.

Soon enough, they chanted his name again.

"Ko-be, Ko-be, Ko-be."

Los Angeles mayor Eric Garcetti spoke for so many with one celebratory tweet Sunday.

"We're back," Garcetti wrote on his official account. "Sweet 17. Thank you @Lakers for bringing it home on a year we needed it. #ForKobe."

Back in the bubble, so far and yet so near, team owner Jeanie Buss stood with the Lakers players,

coaches and staff and delivered a message directly to the franchise's jubilant fans, who had endured so much in 2020 in order to see the promise of the current team fulfilled.

"To Laker Nation, we have been through a heartbreaking tragedy with the loss of our beloved Kobe Bryant and Gianna," Buss said, referring to Bryant's daughter, who also died in the crash. "Let this trophy serve as a reminder that when we come together, believe in each other, incredible things can happen." ∎

MAMBA FOREVER

REMEMBERING KOBE

In Lieu of a Lakers Game, Fans, Hall of Famers Grieve at Staples Center

By Kyle Goon | January 28, 2020

Where there was to be a basketball game, there were dim lights and Hall of Famers sitting in chairs, shedding tears.

Where there was to be cheering, there were silent, empty rows of seats.

Outside Staples Center was where Lakers fans gathered — not in joy, but in grief.

There was only one Kobe Bryant, and mourning his death was a similarly singular affair on Tuesday evening, when the Lakers and Clippers had been previously scheduled to play. The game was postponed out of respect for the Lakers and the Bryant family. In the L.A. Live plaza, thousands of fans, some from as far away as China, roved through memorials of all kinds to the Black Mamba and his daughter, 13-year-old Gianna Bryant, who were among nine to die in a helicopter crash in Calabasas on Sunday morning.

There were eight wall-sized paper murals, erected by the Staples Center staff, tattooed on both sides with personal inscriptions. Hundreds of candles glimmered along metal barriers as the sun set on downtown Los Angeles. There were layers of flowers, purple and golden blossoms, laid down among inscribed jerseys, hats and basketballs. Fans left stuffed animals, balloons, action figures, Kobe Bryant shoes both new and well-worn. People had drawn portraits of Kobe and Gianna, lovingly embracing, or simply printed out pictures and framed.

The grief ran all the way onto the very ground the masses walked on, where messages to Kobe and GiGi were scrawled both in chalk and in ink: "R.I.P. KOBE" or "LEGENDS LIVE FOREVER" or "THANK YOU MAMBA" or "MISS YOU GIGI". Arena officials opened adjacent Chick Hearn Court to pedestrian traffic to allow the placement of still more memorials.

There were those who adopted a game-like atmosphere, chanting "KO-BE" or "M-V-P," and cheering on fans who shot on an office hoop set up on one of the murals. Others sat on the ground or kneeled, uttering prayers or silently weeping.

Most were caught somewhere in between, wandering the makeshift memorials with the readily identifiable haze of grief around them.

Inside Staples Center, that grief was being put into words by people who knew Bryant well. For a TNT special broadcast from center court, former Lakers center Shaquille O'Neal had tears trailing down his cheeks as he spoke about his often fraught relationship with Bryant, who he first met when Kobe was 17 and told him in no uncertain terms that he was going to be the best basketball player ever and "bigger than Will Smith" off the court.

Their three-peat dynasty fueled by the duo was eventually torn apart by their feud. But O'Neal said their names will be forever linked, and he believes that they constituted the "most dominant, big-little, one-two punch ever.

"Got two strong-minded people that are gonna get it done that way," he said. "You're gonna say certain things. The respect will never be lost. But when it comes to being inside the lines and win, that's what we did."

Dwyane Wade talked about how Bryant called him during the 2009 playoffs, asking for advice on how to attack the Celtics' defense. Reggie Miller talked about

Thousands of fans left personalized tributes to Kobe and Gigi Bryant on mural-sized memory boards outside Staples Center. (Pasadena Star-News: Keith Birmingham)

the grudging respect he felt for Bryant after he helped dismantle the Pacers in the 2000 Finals. O'Neal spoke to the loss he felt that he wouldn't be able to speak to Bryant at Kobe's Hall of Fame enshrinement, which is expected to be next fall. He said he hadn't spoken to Bryant since his retirement game in 2016, when Bryant scored 60 points.

"That's the only thing I wish," O'Neal said, "that I could speak to him again."

Jerry West, who famously maneuvered for Bryant after being floored by a workout, said he felt like "his father" when he was running the front office for the Lakers. Although West is now a Clippers consultant, he related a time when Bryant threatened to sign with the Clippers — and West (working for Memphis at the time) talked him out of it, telling him not to play for then-owner Donald Sterling. Even after West left the Lakers in August of 2000, he remained close to Bryant and continued to advise him.

"I don't know if I can get over this," West said, cracking. "I really don't."

That there was no game Tuesday spoke volumes about how the Lakers, and the NBA at large, felt about Bryant's loss.

There's precedent for the NBA canceling games, but they are rarely associated with the death of one person. The league canceled games in 1992 during the Rodney King riots; in 1999 after the Columbine shooting; in 2013 after the Boston Marathon bombing. The last time the NBA is believed to have postponed a game for the death of an individual is in 2000, when Charlotte Hornets player Bobby Phills died in a car collision the day the Hornets were supposed to take on the Chicago Bulls.

Both the Lakers and the Clippers had reservations about staging a game at Staples Center just two days after Bryant's death, two people with knowledge of the situation said. Beyond the readiness of the players, there were also questions about the ability of the hundreds of team employees and arena staff members to be able to work through grief on a short timeline. Bryant was personable and well-known, even after his retirement, and his death left many in the organization devastated.

That was felt at the highest levels: General Manager Rob Pelinka was Bryant's agent for more than a decade before accepting a Lakers role in 2017 and remained close with him — Bryant himself said the two were frequent tennis partners. Team owner Jeanie Buss considered him a close friend and advisor, and The Athletic reported that Bryant was one of the figures who urged her to consolidate her power in the franchise when she fired her brother Jim and longtime GM Mitch Kupchak. ESPN was first to report Pelinka and Buss had gone to Orange County to be with Vanessa Bryant and her surviving children.

Discussions about postponing the game continued through Monday as those in the Lakers organization gauged their emotions, with the team calling in grief counselors on Monday to address employees. In the end, the league and the teams agreed that postponing the game to a later date would be the best strategy for all parties.

Instead of their typical game prep, which would have been a morning shootaround, the Lakers came to their El Segundo practice facility in Tuesday for a light workout and a team luncheon — more for the team to be together than for any functional practice work. The gathering lasted several hours.

Outside of the practice facility were more shrines: A paper mural stretched nearly court-length, with Bryant's face in the middle of each panel. Open bottles of wine and an open can of Modelo were left as offerings among more flowers and candles.

The iron gates of the facility had left a door open for fans to venture in, and here they were more mournful and silent. Purple and gold balloons danced in the wind, and staffers gently picked up vases that had tumbled after particularly strong gusts.

One of the few visitors who spoke was on a video call with a friend, showing the party on the other end of the line the shrine to Bryant and Gianna. She prefaced the display: "Just don't cry, OK?"

Whether you cried or not, you were in good company. ■

The plaza at L.A. Live filled with flowers, candles, balloons and more from grieving Lakers fans. (Pasadena Star-News: Keith Birmingham)

A SALUTE TO MAMBA

Lakers, Fans Honor Kobe Bryant in Emotional Return to Staples Center

By Mirjam Swanson | January 31, 2020

The L.A. Lakers put some basketball on their city's gaping wound Friday.

With thousands of people stationed across the street at a massive memorial, and with thousands more having made their way inside Staples Center, wiping their eyes and cheering in support of their team, the Lakers tipped off for the first time since Kobe Bryant and his 13-year-old daughter Gianna were among nine killed in a helicopter crash in Calabasas.

"Just trying to get through it," Lakers coach Frank Vogel said. "Feeling the same way the rest of the world is, but probably heavier."

The city of Los Angeles mourned its adopted son all week, Bryant's name on the lips of Angelenos everywhere — and graffitied on walls and displayed on Metro's buses and trains.

His two decades of on-court artistry were reflected in murals that sprung up around the city. Bryant's jersey Nos. 8 and 24, which many NBA players chose voluntarily to retire this past week, were put on by legions of regular folk, men and women, many of whom also laced up their Kobe sneakers.

Downtown, where flags outside of the arena hung at half-mast and candles flickered when the sun went down, grieving fans have remained a constant presence at L.A. Live. They've paid their respects by leaving jerseys, basketballs, shoes, flowers and artwork — all of which will be boxed up after Sunday and sent to the Bryant family, at their request, according to Staples Center president Lee Zeidman. He said the flowers would be converted to compost and then spread in planters and garden areas around L.A. Live and Staples Center.

Since Sunday, people have been filling and re-filling every square inch of several garage-door sized boards with testimonials, illustrations and notes of appreciation. Those canvases weren't enough, as sentiments spilled out onto the sidewalk too.

"You were an inspiration. I named my son after you, Kobe."

"I tore my Achilles last year. Thank U for helping me find my stride. I walked here," wrote one fan, alluding to Bryant's late-career injury, from which he returned to retire as the third-leading scorer in NBA history with 33,643 points.

"Thank you, Kobe, for the LOVE OF BASKETBALL."

Bryant was an 18-time All-Star who won five NBA championships and became one of the greatest basketball players of his generation during his 20-year career, all of it spent with the Lakers.

He nicknamed himself the Black Mamba and inspired devotion — or at least respect, from his adversaries — with his relentless, hard-edged work ethic.

"It feels like a family member passed away," said Carlos Villasenor, who visited the site Friday in a replica of Bryant's maroon Lower Merion No. 33 high school jersey.

"It's one of those things, we didn't really know him or meet him, but he touched a lot of people's hearts. Just with his hustle on the court, too. That spilled out to everybody else and influences everybody else to just hustle and play. Doesn't matter what you're doing in life, whatever job that you have, you have to have that energy that you put into it, that focus, whatever you're doing."

Bryant's former Lakers teammate Luke Walton visited L.A. Live around 2 a.m. on Thursday, in town as coach of the Sacramento Kings, who played the Clippers that night. He was taken by hearing fans chanting "Koooh-bee!" in the middle of the night.

Those chants made their way inside Staples Center — where many of Bryant's most storied moments

LeBron James, center, and his Lakers teammates are overcome with emotion during the pre-game tribute to Kobe Bryant. (Daily Breeze: Scott Varley)

occurred, including his 81-point game on Jan. 22, 2006 — before the Lakers' game Friday against the Portland Trail Blazers, where roses were left on two courtside seats, chairs draped with jerseys representing Kobe and Gianna, who was an emerging basketball sensation.

A yellow T-shirt with either a purple and white No. 8 or No. 24 was placed on every other seat in the arena.

Inside, "Ko-be" chants were interspersed with "M-V-P" and "Gigi" chants during a pregame tribute that included a 24.2-second moment of silence and a rendition of "Amazing Grace" from Usher.

Boyz II Men, the soul group from Bryant's native Philadelphia sang the national anthem that ended with several of the Lakers players in tears.

And then LeBron James, the Lakers' current superstar leader, delivered a message — not from a script, which he ditched, but from his heart.

"As I look around this area, we're all grieving, we're all hurt, we are all heartbroken," James said. "And when we're going through things like this, the best thing you can do is lean on the shoulders of your family.

"Now, I heard about Lakers Nation before I got here last year," he continued, "about how much of a family it is. And that is absolutely what I've seen this whole week, not only from the players, not only from the coaching staff, not only from the organization, but from everybody. Everybody that's here, this is really, truly, truly a family." ■

'FOREVER AND ALWAYS'

Kobe and Gigi Bryant Remembered in Intimate Details by Closest Friends and Family

By Kyle Goon | February 24, 2020

The world knew him as the Black Mamba, a brilliant and relentless competitor and an aspiring entertainment mogul. But there were sides of Kobe Bryant most could never see.

The "little brother" who texted Michael Jordan at odd hours to talk about footwork and the triangle offense. The "best friend" who played tireless rounds of tennis with Rob Pelinka and greeted his children with a loving embrace. The "soulmate" who made extravagant gestures for his wife, including buying the movie prop notebook and Rachel McAdams' dress from the romantic film, "The Notebook." And the "girl dad" who consulted the best minds in basketball as he set to coach his daughter's team.

These were the sides of Kobe Bryant, and by extension, his daughter Gianna Bryant, that were revealed even to some of his most ardent fans on Monday as both were memorialized in a "Celebration of Life" ceremony at Staples Center. It was the most intimate look the many millions of mourners across the world have ever gotten at the Lakers legend and his family, whose larger-than-life public image was brought down to earth with revealing stories by those who knew him best.

There were no words more powerful than those of Vanessa Bryant, the grieving wife and mother who spoke for the first time since Kobe (age 41), Gianna (age 13) and seven others were killed in a helicopter crash in Calabasas a month ago.

She described her daughter as "pure joy," a bright pupil who knew multiple languages and loved to bake, and a goofy, caring sister to her three surviving siblings, Natalia, Bianka and Capri. She called Kobe a doting husband who had plans to travel the world with her and become "fun grandparents."

It was a starkly personal portrait: She told stories of how Gianna would kiss her every day, even when she was asleep after long nights with newborns. She recited all the pet names she and Kobe called each other, and how she and the girls playfully chastised him after the first time he was late picking them up from school in his retirement. Her voice cracked as she talked about Gianna's smile, which took up her whole face, and her laughter: "It was infectious, it was pure and genuine."

She lingered, painfully, on the moments that she will never get to see with either of them — driving lessons, college and weddings among them — but took whatever small measure of comfort she could that they were together at the end.

"God knew they couldn't be on this earth without each other," she said. "He had to bring them home to have them together."

The event featured moving addresses from some of Bryant's most accomplished peers, like Jordan and Shaquille O'Neal. There were also speeches from WNBA star Diana Taurasi, Oregon phenom Sabrina Ionescu and UConn coach Geno Auriemma, representing some of the brightest luminaries in women's basketball where Gianna hoped to make her mark.

An event attended by both basketball stars and high-wattage entertainment figures also featured musical numbers by Beyoncé, Alicia Keys and Christina Aguilera, representing the scope of Bryant's impact and the depth of his loss. The grief poured out

Vanessa Bryant recalls her life with Kobe and Gianna during the memorial at Staples Center. (Southern California News Group: David Crane)

like the 33,643 roses enveloping the main stage — one for every point he scored in his NBA career.

"When Kobe Bryant died, a piece of me died," Jordan said. "And as I look in this arena and across the globe, a piece of you died. Or else you wouldn't be here."

The stature Bryant achieved in life was represented in part by the attendees who gathered on the floor of Staples Center, where he built his career on the hardwood, and how many of those figures showed their grief as the ceremony proceeded. Many of the NBA stars who attended — James Harden, Russell Westbrook, Anthony Davis — wore dark glasses even in the low-lit arena, hiding reddened and tear-stained eyes. Others, like Phil Jackson and father Joe Bryant, were shown on screen with their eyes shut in solemn meditation.

Even the day's host, Jimmy Kimmel, found it difficult to keep from stammering as he made his opening comments and read the name of the crash victims. Words caught in his throat from the beginning: "I don't think any of us could have imagined this — everywhere you go, you see his face, his number, Gigi's face, Gigi's number, everywhere, at every intersection."

The intimate tone was set from the beginning: As fans who were lucky enough to get tickets through the online selection process streamed in the door, they were given Bryant-themed shirts and pins. They were also given a 30-page booklet that felt much like a family photo album, with some well-known images of Bryant as a Laker spliced alongside shots of the Bryants during holidays or together at Disneyland. In the arena, as performers prepared, a video of Gianna's basketball highlights — and some of Alyssa Altobelli and Payton Chester who also died in the crash — played accompanied by hip-hop tracks.

The world heard from people close enough to text and call Kobe: Pelinka described their final exchange when Kobe asked him to help secure an internship for Alexis Altobelli, the surviving daughter of John and Keri Altobelli killed in the crash with her sister Alyssa. He had sent the message early on the fatal flight.

"Kobe's last human act was to use his platform to bless and shape a young girl's future," Pelinka said. "Hasn't Kobe done that for all of us?"

Ionescu, who Kobe had mentored and who had worked out with Gianna, said she still texts Kobe's number. Sometimes she finds herself hoping she will hear back.

Jordan, whose tears at his Hall of Fame speech launched an unstoppable meme, had the wherewithal to recognize the irony that another one of his rare public appearances again caught him weeping. But he spun it back into a tribute, saying that Bryant was one of the few people ever who could get under his skin.

While he was at times frustrated that Bryant would call him at all hours of the night, wanting to discuss minutiae such as his footwork or complaining about Phil Jackson and the triangle offense. But over time, Jordan came to see Bryant as his "little brother," and they talked about all kinds of things, including business and their families. Jordan said over time, "that nuisance turned into love."

"That is what Kobe Bryant does to me," Jordan said, a smile creeping across his wet cheeks. "He knows how to get to you in a way that affects you personally. Even if he's being a pain in the ass. But you always have a sense of love for him, and the way he can bring out the best in you. And he did that for me."

His Airness also provided one of the day's most graceful unscripted moments: He offered Vanessa his supporting hand as she stepped down from the stage.

The solemnity of the occasion was broken up by occasional, much-needed levity. Shaq offered a story when he said he told Kobe to pass because there was no "I" in "team," which provoked a retort: "I know, but there's an 'M-E' in that (expletive). Auriemma hammered a similar joke home, saying when he saw Gianna pass when she was open: "I thought, 'She's not listening to her father.'"

There was also some inspiration: The event itself raised money for the Mamba and Mambacita Sports Foundation, which seeks to extend equal opportunities in youth sports. That issue has seen raised visibility in the wake of the crash, where the occupants were on

Michael Jordan delivers a tearful farewell to Kobe Bryant, whom he considered "a little brother." (Southern California News Group: David Crane)

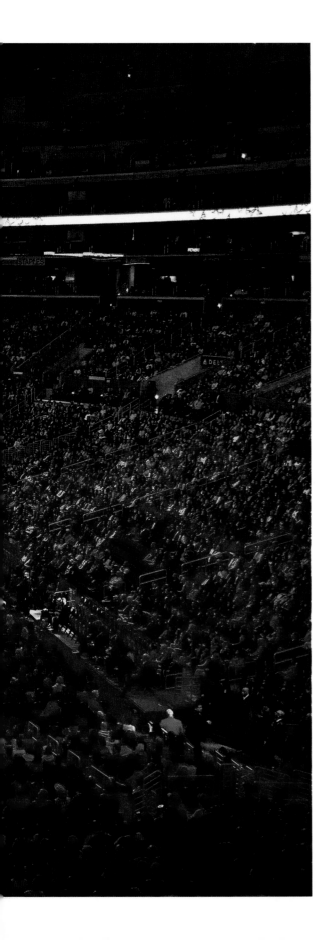

their way to a youth basketball tournament at Bryant's Mamba Academy in Thousand Oaks.

Vanessa told about how Gianna wrote a school paper how the pay gap between the NBA and WNBA was unfair, a cause that certainly is a passionate one among the WNBA, which just negotiated a new labor agreement last year. While her dream of becoming a WNBA star will never be realized, there was hope that her example will serve as inspiration to others who have that same dream — or would support those who do.

"Gigi in many ways represents the future of women's basketball — a future in which a young woman aspires to play in the WNBA the same way I wanted to be a Laker," Taurasi said. "She represents a time where a young girl doesn't need permission to play. Her skill would command respect."

But largely, the event felt like a final farewell to the people whose deaths have cast a shadow over the Lakers, the NBA, Southern California and beyond the last few weeks. The Laker players were given the day off, and they showed up for the ceremony to grieve. Other team employees caught a morning bus from the El Segundo practice facility to be present in the arena.

Among the many former teammates and on-court opposition Bryant faced in his career were Lamar Odom, Pau Gasol, Steve Nash, Rick Fox, Derek Fisher and the bulk of the San Antonio Spurs dynasty that served as one of his great foils. Jennifer Lopez and Alex Rodriguez sat in the same row as Vanessa and her children, along with team owner Jeanie Buss, and after singing "XO" and "Halo," two of Kobe's favorite songs, Beyoncé sat behind Vanessa and squeezed her shoulder during the day's difficult moments.

It was a celebration, as friends and family had hoped. But it was also, inescapably, goodbye.

"We love you both and miss you," Vanessa said. "Forever and always." ∎

An image of Kobe and Gianna Bryant is displayed on the scoreboard at their Staples Center memorial service. (Southern California News Group: David Crane)

PRESSING PAUSE

NBA Suspends Season After Player Tests Positive for Coronavirus

By Kyle Goon | March 11, 2020

After a week of ramping intensity in the threat of the coronavirus, the NBA season came to a screeching halt on Wednesday night.

After Utah Jazz center Rudy Gobert tested positive for COVID-19, a planned game between the Jazz and the Oklahoma City Thunder was immediately halted moments before tip-off. Within an hour, the NBA had suspended the season indefinitely with no clear plan forward in an unprecedented health crisis for the league.

"The NBA is suspending game play following the conclusion of tonight's schedule of games until further notice," the league said in a statement. "The NBA will use this hiatus to determine next steps for moving forward in regard to the coronavirus pandemic."

It could be a watershed moment — not just for the NBA, but for sporting events at large. The NBA is the first of the major professional U.S. sports leagues to suspend all games, forced to skip half-measures by the positive test of a player.

The NBA said Gobert, a two-time Defensive Player of the Year from France, was not present in the arena during the game. The positive test result came in shortly before tip-off, sending medical staffers rushing to the court to usher players back into their locker rooms. A half-hour later the Chesapeake Energy Arena public address announcer informed those in the arena that the game had been postponed.

Locally, the Lakers had a game scheduled Thursday night against the Houston Rockets and announced that fans would be able to receive refunds for tickets from point of purchase. The Clippers were scheduled for a Friday home game against the Nets.

Now for the foreseeable future, there will be no basketball in Staples Center.

The league had spent much of the early week contemplating measures to rein in the spread of the virus, which has nearly 125,000 confirmed cases worldwide and more than 4,500 associated deaths. After closing locker rooms to non-essential personnel to lower player risk, the NBA's governors had discussed a number of possibilities to limit fan exposure: ESPN reported many of the league's owners in a Wednesday discussion were in favor of playing games without fans — a step many other sporting events, including the NCAA Tournament, had already announced.

The stakes escalated quickly: Earlier in the day, players and coaches had openly discussed the possibility of playing without fans after the Golden State Warriors had announced they intended to play their game Thursday night closed to the public.

"I mean, it's surreal," Lakers coach Frank Vogel said of closed-door games, hours before the sudden test. "But it's something that we knew was probably coming and it's unfortunate and hopefully not long-lasting."

The positive COVID-19 test blew away all earlier hopes that the NBA would be able to continue without fans. The Boston Herald reported that teams that had faced the Jazz over the last 10 days were being asked to self-quarantine. In the previous week-and-a-half, the Jazz had played road games in Cleveland, New York, Boston and Detroit before hosting Toronto at home. A planned game between the New Orleans Pelicans and Sacramento Kings was called off on Wednesday in Sacramento, with local media reporting that players became alarmed once they learned Courtney Kirkland, who officiated the March 9 game between the Jazz and Raptors, would be in the referee crew.

The South Bay Lakers played a home game Wednesday night in El Segundo, a win over the

Video screens broadcast images of Los Angeles Lakers' Anthony Davis to an empty plaza as the NBA season remained suspended. (AP Images)

Austin Spurs before the NBA also announced the G League season had been suspended.

In Oklahoma City, players and staffers from both the Thunder and Jazz were reportedly being tested for coronavirus and were held in their respective locker rooms long after fans had left. ESPN reported that the Jazz would be quarantined in Oklahoma City for now. Other people who had come into contact with Gobert, including traveling media members, were expected to stay in place until they could be tested.

Mavericks owner Mark Cuban spoke to reporters in Dallas, telling ESPN that teams would be able to continue to practice.

Players learned on social media that the season would be suspended and responded in kind. From his "Inside The Green Room" podcast social media account, Lakers guard Danny Green recorded a video statement wishing those affected by COVID-19 a speedy recovery.

"Obviously it sucks. It's unfortunate," he said. "We want to continue to play basketball. The fans want to continue to watch basketball. And we want to continue to entertain you guys as best we can. But these are the right steps we need to take. The NBA's making the right call. And hopefully, we get it back up and running in the right direction soon."

Even before the decision was announced, players had treated Gobert's test with caution. "If you're gonna take precautions … take all the precautions," Clippers guard Lou Williams tweeted at 5:40 p.m., before the decision Wednesday.

Lakers veteran Jared Dudley had tweeted: "I personally would rather postpone to make sure we can finally get ahead of this virus."

After the news broke Wednesday evening, the Lakers were in the process of gathering more information before issuing a statement on behalf of the organization. The Clippers canceled a scheduled practice and said they would follow up as more information became available.

The Lakers canceled a Thursday morning shootaround but allowed players to come in for treatment if they wished. Team employees were asked to work from home if possible. ■

RESTED AND READY

Lakers Focus on Player Health and Injury Prevention Ahead of Restart

By Kyle Goon | July 2, 2020

For just about four months, Anthony Davis lived with the pain.

After an injury during the opening slate of games last fall when he jammed his right shoulder, it was common, even for months afterward, to see the 6-foot-10 forward rolling the joint while wincing in pain. Davis gets these nagging injuries that are difficult to shake once in the rhythm of the season.

So in one light, the hiatus has done him good: Without the physical toll of games and going through daily workouts — with plenty of down time with video games mixed in — Davis said Thursday he feels as good as he's felt physically all year.

"It's been good for me to kind of let some of them lingering injuries I had towards the time when the NBA stopped to kind of recover and heal and get back into the best version of myself," he said. "I feel 100 percent healthy. Well, I don't feel — I am."

Keeping Davis and the other Lakers that way is a priority for the team, which has zeroed in on staying healthy headed to the NBA's Orlando restart later this month. While the threat of COVID-19 looms over all the proceedings, the Lakers anticipate that the abbreviated timeline to get back into shape and the unusual circumstances of play could mean the NBA title will be won by the team that can withstand the most attrition.

To that end, the Lakers will be sending a full roster of 17 players, including two-way contract players Devontae Cacok and Kostas Antetokounmpo, to provide maximum depth. NBA teams are restricted to a 35-person initial travel party, which coach Frank Vogel said the Lakers will use heavily on medical staff at the expense of some spots for coaches.

While the Lakers have not disclosed which coaches will not be traveling to Orlando on July 9, Vogel said "miserable" decisions were necessary to protect the health of the players.

"Just because of the history of players coming back after a lockout types of situations and the high risk of injury," he said. "Additionally, with the COVID protocols and potentially having guys out, we did decide to bring 17 players so that we make sure that we have enough practice bodies. What that does is it leaves you, and what most teams are going through, it leaves you a little bit shorthanded on the coaching front."

Coaches who don't travel with the team initially will work remotely, and as long as the Lakers advance through the postseason, they anticipate more staffers will be able to join the campus.

For the time being, all of the Lakers' work is focused on their bodies. Between the weight room, training room and court time, players have a lot to squeeze in roughly two-hour windows at the practice facility. Vogel said he prefers giving them more time now to spend with their families: The Lakers will dive more into film and group work when they arrive in Orlando and clear quarantine.

Game-ready shape requires physicality, speed and reaction ability that Vogel said many players haven't truly tested in months.

"All those types of things have been dormant, so to speak," he said. "They've just gotta be, hopefully, brought back in a relatively quick fashion and at the right pace. We're very concerned about going too fast once we get going."

While Avery Bradley is sitting out the restart and Dwight Howard is still reportedly mulling his options and could join the Lakers later in the

Anthony Davis looks to pass the ball against the Los Angeles Clippers during the Lakers' first game in the NBA bubble. (AP Images)

process, Davis said he's had no reservations about getting back to competition. The NBA announced Thursday morning that nine new positive COVID cases surfaced among players, and 848 tests of traveling staffers revealed 10 new COVID cases.

Vogel and Davis said they trust the league's preparation and guidelines, and they believe attendees will follow the restrictions of the Disney World campus for the greater good.

"Obviously the numbers are spiking in Orlando, and I don't think no one wants to get COVID," Davis said. "So I don't think guys would put themselves, or hopefully won't put themselves, the other players and staff that's gonna be in the bubble in jeopardy."

The steady rise in cases around the country is just one of the uncertain factors the Lakers face, along with losing Bradley and not being sure Howard will join. They'll also seek to continue blending Markieff Morris and Dion Waiters, as well as new signee J.R. Smith. Between the age of the roster and the quick uptick to the July 30 start, there could be increased risk of injury for the Lakers as much as any team.

And yet Davis seemed confident that his team remains the one everyone is trying to unseat.

"Actually, I think our chances are higher just because we're all rested and we're all ready to go," he said. "If anything, our chances got higher and it's going to be about just who wants it more. Everybody kind of had a decompression of the season and obviously with stuff going on, but it's about what team wants it more and which team can stay healthy." ∎

WALKING THE WALK

LeBron James Showed He Was Willing to Leave, and the NBA was Worried

By Kyle Goon | August 27, 2020

When the bubble was created, the wide speculation was that LeBron James had the most to lose.

After two topsy-turvy years, the Lakers had assembled a championship contender. At 35, James could be at the very edge of his prime. As a storm brewed in June, with players openly discussing sitting out of the restart to focus solely on social justice issues, James made known that he would do something, but that he was also ready to play.

So when he walked out of the Coronado Springs Resort ballroom on Wednesday night after making the case that NBA players should sit out the rest of the season, it created shockwaves that threatened to pop the bubble itself.

The Milwaukee Bucks made a powerful statement on Wednesday afternoon that the racism that plagues America is too great to let stand. It made sense that a team from Wisconsin, where the shooting of Jacob Blake occurred, and a team that has experienced disproportionate aggression from law enforcement itself, would be the one to make the stand that had been buzzing around the bubble for two days.

But even as this blindsided a number of the NBA's most powerful figures, there was a sense of security in the idea that teams like the Lakers and stars like James would probably take up their same June position and move for the season to continue.

But apparently this was miscalculation: James understands the unique position he's in, and compared to other players, he also has a lot less to lose. He doesn't need the money that he would make in the playoffs as badly as others in the league do. He also has a platform that is cultural — if basketball stops, people will still pay attention to LeBron James and what he has to say, because his celebrity and influence transcend a normal athlete's. Before players agreed to resume the season on Thursday morning, the NBA felt more precarious than ever because the one pin they never thought would be pulled suddenly felt shaky.

On Wednesday, James wielded this cudgel deftly. The Athletic reported he asked for more from the team owners, who committed $300 million over the next 10 years to economic empowerment in Black communities. He also reportedly took issue with commissioner Adam Silver, who has not been within the innermost tier of the bubble.

But those words don't have the same impact unless James is willing to walk.

Several Lakers did want to play, sources told Southern California News Group, and several players wanted not only to win a championship, but to continue to use basketball as a platform to speak out on injustices. But they also haven't been willing to go against James, and whatever he wanted to do, they were going to ride alongside him.

Sources said that the Lakers felt angst toward Milwaukee, and that the player meeting became contentious after coaches were asked to leave midway through. That while the Bucks did use the moment to call Wisconsin state leaders and demand reform, they thought that Milwaukee's decision was more impulsive than planned out, and they wished to see a longer-term impactful strategy to hold others more accountable.

When the Lakers and Clippers endorsed walking out, it was Miami's Udonis Haslem who posed a

LeBron James kneels during the national anthem before a rescheduled Game 5 against the Portland Trail Blazers. (AP Images)

rhetorical question to the group: Can the postseason even be legitimate without those two teams and the stars on them?

To understand James, it's worth looking at his record, especially in light of comments made by White House senior advisor Jared Kushner, who said of NBA players: "But I think that what we need to do is turn that from slogans and signals to actual action that's going to solve the problem." To suggest that NBA players, and James as much as anyone, haven't tried to solve the problem is not just inaccurate, but willfully disingenuous.

For at least eight years, James has been politically outspoken on the use of lethal force against Black people, memorably in a picture shared by the Miami Heat wearing hoodies after the shooting of Trayvon Martin in 2012. James began to realize at that time the importance of speaking out as his sons were growing to an age where their lives could be threatened by virtue of being Black.

This work has sprawled into work on numerous fronts in creating lasting change in Black communities. He's helped fund college scholarships for students to go to the University of Akron provided they meet certain grade and community service criteria. He's built an actual public school, I Promise in Akron, with the goal of serving children who need support well beyond the classroom — a model that has been admired across the country and could one day be replicated. That school also now includes housing for families of students who experience homelessness, which is probably even more important in a pandemic with people losing jobs due to COVID-19.

He's most recently founded More Than A Vote, which is pouring money and effort into various voting initiatives, including trying to encourage more young people to become election poll workers since older workers are more susceptible to COVID-19.

But the other side of James has embraced the more fiery political discourse, stemming from public clashes with president Donald Trump that resulted in conservative talk show host Laura Ingraham telling him to "Shut up and dribble."

That 2018 instance marked a turning point in James' media brand. His company, Uninterrupted, funneled money into sports documentaries about activist athletes, including a series actually called "Shut Up And Dribble," appropriating Ingraham's words to his own ends. He is an admirer of Muhammad Ali, whose stance against the Vietnam war cost him prime years in his career, and he funded a documentary about Ali, too.

James' social activism efforts have been widely praised, but he also puts himself in the crosshairs for criticism for those who do not agree with him politically. Just like on the court, when James fails to meet his own high standard, he receives a great deal of backlash — such as in October when he criticized Houston Rockets GM Daryl Morey tweets about Hong Kong for being "misinformed," then later backtracked.

But even in less controversial stances, James is the subject of all manner of vile criticism that is largely based on racism. A Lakers team source who has had his social media accounts referenced by James' own said he has felt, particularly since June, that many have sent messages of race-based hatred as James continues to advocate for Black Lives.

"I can only imagine what he sees every day," the source told SCNG.

Yahoo Sports reported that James changed positions sometime between Wednesday night and Thursday morning, perhaps recognizing that many NBA players who have informed and important things to say about social justice need the platform the NBA provides.

The Athletic also reported that walking away from the season would have profound and difficult ramifications for most players, including the end of the current Collective Bargaining Agreement. A renegotiation would likely wind up with owners trying to recoup their losses by taking more of the players' share. While many NBA players are wealthy, few (and probably none) are as wealthy as James.

If James did experience a dramatic change of heart, it was probably out of recognition of those who don't have as many resources as he does — a principle that animates his leadership in the league, but also his charity. But it's also worth pointing out that even a brief moment of suspense pushed the league to the brink, because no one makes the NBA hold its breath like LeBron James. ∎

LeBron James' activism in recent years has expanded to opening the I Promise school in Akron, Ohio. (AP Images)

23

SMALL FORWARD

LEBRON JAMES

In the Bubble, LeBron James' Routines and Team Bonds Have Kept Him and Lakers on Track

By Kyle Goon | September 29, 2020

In the most rigid routines, small deviations appear like gulfs.

LeBron James is a man of regimen. He likes to arrive on the first bus to the arena on game nights. He sleeps "more than anyone I know," said Anthony Davis, with some players whispering that can be up to 15 hours in a day. He ices his knees and his feet — a timer goes off, as scripted to let him know exactly how many seconds he needs to spend wrapped in the cold.

Phil Handy knows the rigidity of James' rhythms well: The Lakers assistant also worked with James for four years in Cleveland, each one of them a Finals run. This year he's been the on-court coach who warms up the 35-year-old in his 17th season. If anyone would see the cracks in the system, it would be him — but Handy swears he doesn't.

"His energy is so consistent," Handy said. "Every time he steps on the court, I can't remember a time I've looked at him and said, 'He doesn't have it tonight.'"

Of course James has had off nights in the NBA bubble — but three-quarters of the way through a playoff run, they've been the exception, not the rule. His Lakers are 12-3, cutting through the Blazers, Rockets and Nuggets and poised to win the franchise's 17th title and his fourth if they can top the Miami Heat. A triumphant Game 5 to close out the Nuggets in the conference finals showed that James' will to compete is still standing the test of time.

He's scoring less than he did in his last postseason appearance two years ago but shooting better and rebounding more. He's not far off a triple-double average in postseason play (26.7 ppg, 10.3 rpg, 8.9 apg), even though he's averaging a career-low 35 minutes per game. The Lakers have outscored opponents by 129 points when he's on the floor.

It's been a resurgence of the quasi-mythic "Playoff LeBron," a strict, serious and focused competitor who thrives on fanatical discipline to routine. But how does one keep everything the same in the bubble, where in James' own words, "nothing is normal"?

It's a riddle with contradictory evidence. Most teammates would tell you little has changed, that James has the same approach he always has. But James

LeBron James goes for a dunk during a regular season game against the Portland Trail Blazers (Daily Breeze: Scott Varley)

himself has hinted how much the conditions of the bubble have bothered him in bits and pieces. During the seeding games, he deferred comment on "some things that you really can't control that's here, that I really don't want to talk about that's kinda like off the floor," and after the late August stoppage, he joked he thought about leaving the bubble "once a day."

A man who has made a career of trying to cover over his weak spots and intimidate and fluster opponents acknowledged on the eve of his 10th Finals series that playing through the bubble might rank up as his most difficult feat.

"It's probably been the most challenging thing I've ever done as far as a professional, as far as committing to something and actually making it through," he said. "I would be lying if I sat up here and knew that everything inside the bubble, the toll that it would take on your mind and your body and everything else, because it's been extremely tough."

While "Playoff LeBron" has been in many ways a similar character, winning games and similar ways and putting his body through similar routines, James has had to adapt — he's found tweaks to his postseason rhythms to get the same results.

"His attention to detail is off the charts, to every series, every game," Davis said. "He's locked in as soon as he steps into the arena. Takes care of his body. He sleeps more than anybody I know. So those things, like the things he does now — he has all this recovery stuff shipped in and stuff like that, but it's why he's been so dominant for 17 years."

James' attention to his body has a certain mystique, especially given that he reportedly spends up to $1.5 million annually on training, recovery and diet. Several Lakers asked about equipment he shipped in said they didn't know all of James' tech — he did reveal himself on Instagram that one of the items he brought in was a hyperbaric chamber, meant to increase oxygen flow and possibly promote healing.

But so much of what James does is simply committing the hours. He blocks out his sleep, getting at least eight hours every night and strictly adhering to a pregame nap. J.R. Smith said at shootarounds, James tells teammates exactly when he's going to bed and when he'll wake up. When he gets to his hotel after games, he'll work hours afterward with trainer Mike Mancias on treatment and therapy before bed.

It helped get James, who admitted in July he wasn't where he wanted to be physically, into shape. Ferocious dunks and chase down blocks are back in his repertoire after a few early weeks of trying to get his legs back underneath him.

Teammates have seen shadows of this routine throughout the season and maybe catch him up late at the practice facility, Alex Caruso said, but in the bubble, they've gained more appreciation for how thorough James' process really is. Davis said taking on some of James' advice has helped him go from a player once notorious for his frequent trips to the locker room to playing one of the healthiest stretches of his career.

Even small things don't get cut. Assistant coach Jason Kidd noted that in an arena without showers, many players are in a rush to get back to their hotel rooms. James takes the time to ice up. He saw it when they were teammates in the 2008 Olympics but seeing the discipline over the course of a full year has given him more appreciation.

"Now as a coach, it's just impressive, the detail of work he does and that he's not bored," he said. "You have to give him kudos for that, because it's easy in this atmosphere to take shortcuts."

That means film, too. James said he watched every minute of the playoffs last season, and he's famously voracious. While he likes to end his nights by playing Madden and drinking a glass of wine, he

LeBron James warms up before facing the Rockets in the Western Conference Semifinals. While James admitted he was not at peak fitness entering the bubble, his discipline and commitment led to stellar numbers in the playoffs. (AP Images)

also told Southern California News Group that film of opponents will run in the background.

"I've changed it up a lot, but this right here and my preparation has been the same," he said. "I sit in my room, I watch the film, and sometimes it's just sitting on the TV just on a loop."

It seems that James has been grounded by these familiar game routines. But the social media blackout he's had for some postgame runs was a non-starter, in part because of his More Than A Vote initiative that he wants to help promote: "I've got some (expletive) off the floor that I'm working on as well coming November, so I couldn't afford to go quiet."

Family is another issue. He told SCNG that not seeing his three children for the last three months has been "extreme," and without FaceTime to see them, he would have doubts about the ability to make it through the bubble.

What has helped, he said, is living along the same hallway at the Gran Destino Hotel with his team. Wherever he's gone, James has tried to build college-like culture. He describes his Miami years, when he played for the Heat between 25 and 29, as his "college," which taught him how to win and build camaraderie. Subsequent efforts have not always succeeded, but this 2019-20 has that build.

"We're together more than we're with our families. … Who else you gonna be with?" he said. "And if it's not organic, then it's gonna feel forced. Our team, we love being around each other. It's crazy."

During the regular season, the Lakers were close off the court, whether going to JaVale McGee's ugly sweater party, or donning suits for James' 35th birthday, or renting out the back room of a New York restaurant in January. The darker side of this bond came through a collective trauma: learning that Kobe Bryant had died during a cross-country flight from Philadelphia to Los Angeles. That event and the

difficult weeks and months that followed bound the teammates closer, as they shared tearful stories about Bryant and locked arms in an emotional return to Staples Center.

On the bubble campus, the close quarters created a dorm-like environment that James helped fill by organizing a Madden video game tournament. The Lakers have pizza or pool parties on the occasional off-day. They sometimes watch games together. After the Western Conference Finals win on Saturday, they threw a party at the Three Bridges Restaurant that carried past 4 a.m.

"This is probably the tightest group I've ever seen in this short of a span," said Smith, a veteran of James' Cavalier teams who joined the Lakers just in June. "Obviously the bubble takes into it, but we've got a lot of veteran guys who have either been there before or trying to get it done. And it just makes it that much easier with the personalities we've got. Everyone knows what they're here for, everyone's easygoing."

James is not there for all the team activities — Smith said he went golfing twice with the group, and it rained both times. But the underlying sense of camaraderie has been motivating, too, giving him a reason to stick with the regimen that's helped him be this successful for so long.

There's a certain trickle-down effect that James' mood can influence his locker room. The greatest feat Handy has seen is that whatever anxieties and struggles James might be having in the bubble, when he goes into practice, when he goes to the court, or when he lines up for tip-off, he still doesn't see the fissures.

He simply sees LeBron James, ready to work.

"Whatever challenges, you never hear about it, you don't talk about it, he doesn't use them as excuses," Handy said. "Everybody who is in here is dealing with some challenge. He knows that, and he sets the table for us to have success." ■

LeBron James poses for a photo during Lakers media day in September 2019. More than a year later, in unprecedented circumstances, James and the Lakers would triumph in the NBA Finals. (Daily Breeze: Scott Varley)

3

POWER FORWARD

ANTHONY DAVIS

This is Why Anthony Davis is a Laker

By Jim Alexander | September 20, 2020

The seeds of Sunday night's madness in the Orlando bubble, and the latest addition to the Laker franchise's gallery of postseason moments, were planted June 15, 2019. That was the day the Lakers landed Anthony Davis from the New Orleans Pelicans, the day Davis and LeBron James got their wishes, and the day that sometimes quixotic quest for the franchise's 17th title again got serious.

"This," Davis told TNT's Allie LaForce Sunday evening, "is what they brought me here for."

Davis' buzzer-beating three-pointer — officially a 26-footer according to the play-by-play sheet — for a 105-103 victory over Denver didn't win a championship or even a series. There is still way too much work to do during this Western Conference Finals showdown with the stubborn Nuggets, never mind anything beyond that.

But given the circumstances — down a point, 2.1 seconds left when the ball was inbounded, against a team that has established it has no quit in it — this may have been the most inspiring L.A. walkoff since

... well, you've got Kirk Gibson's home run in 1988, Alec Martinez' Stanley Cup-winning goal for the Kings in 2014, Derek Fisher with 0.4 seconds left in San Antonio in 2004, Robert Horry's shot to beat Sacramento in 2002 and Tyus Edney going the length of the floor for UCLA against Missouri in 1995. Not too many others leap to mind.

Not to brag, but I wrote it last summer, the day the trade went down:

"This is what the Lakers should be doing. It's part of their DNA ... (It) tells their fans and their city that this franchise still means business, even if there is still reason to question their front office structure."

Nobody is questioning it now, of course. Moments like this — and in fact a season like this, elongated as it has been — have created a collective amnesia about those seven seasons in the playoff desert, those years when we sometimes weren't sure exactly what the Lakers stood for beyond the gauzy memories of the past.

Games and series like this remind us of what that franchise does stand for. And there is but one regret about this particular buzzer-beater.

Anthony Davis rises toward the hoop during a regular season match-up against the Milwaukee Bucks. (AP Images)

"The one thing I wish A.D. had tonight with the shot that he made, I wish we were playing at Staples," LeBron James said. "I mean, we miss our fans so much. And I can only imagine. It probably would have blew the roof off Staples Center, A.D. hitting that shot tonight in Staples with our crowd. I would have loved for him to have that moment, because I know what it felt like for me."

James' reference was to Game 2 of the 2009 Eastern Conference finals, when he hit a 25-footer with no time left, at home, to give Cleveland a 96-95 win over an Orlando team led by current Laker teammate Dwight Howard. But I suppose we should stop that comparison right there, because Orlando won that series in six (en route to losing in the Finals to the, um, Lakers).

Davis wanted this type of pressure, and this type of responsibility. That's why he forced his way out of New Orleans. The Pelicans got to the second round once while he was there, but there was no assurance that it was going to get any better.

"Just because his teams haven't been good enough to reach this moment (before now) doesn't mean that he's not that caliber of player," Lakers coach Frank Vogel said. "We saw that tonight. No surprise (to) me. No surprise (to) our whole group."

There were no guarantees in L.A., either, when he arrived. But Davis teaming up with James provided the 1-2 punch that enabled Rob Pelinka to fill in around them, and the general manager has gone from presumed doofus to an Executive of the Year candidate – and I'd assume inquiries about his ring size – as a result.

The shot Davis made Sunday night was similar to one he took in the Lakers' last pre-pandemic game, a three-pointer in front of the visitors bench with time running out against Brooklyn on March 10. That one he missed, in a 104-102 loss.

"LeBron will tell you," Davis recalled. "I mean, probably the first four days I was like, 'Damn, I should have made that shot. I've got to make that shot.' He said, 'You're fine, you're fine.'

"But I put more pressure on myself than anybody. I feel like every shot I take is supposed to go in, and I have enough confidence in my shot to make those type of plays."

This one, he acknowledged, was the biggest of his career, and his first buzzer-beater for a victory. Again, that's why he's here.

"When I left (New Orleans) I just wanted to compete for a championship, and I know that moments like this come with it, especially in L.A., the biggest market in basketball," he said.

It's part of the Lakers legacy. And so is this: The Lakers wore their "Mamba Black" uniforms Sunday night, and Vogel was caught on the telecast telling his team it was a "Mamba shot," one that Kobe Bryant would hit.

"We just play a little different" in those jerseys," Davis said. "Our swagger is a little different. Every time we put on those jerseys, we're representing him.

"Coach made sure we knew that in the huddle. He said, 'Look at the jerseys you have on. He would have made big-time plays. So it's time for us to make big-time plays.' "

Done. ■

Anthony Davis soars to block Damian Lillard's shot during the Lakers' first-round playoff series against the Portland Trail Blazers. (AP Images)

THROUGH THE STORM

Lakers Owner Jeanie Buss Reflects with Pride on a Long, Strange, Difficult Season

By Kyle Goon | October 8, 2020

There are times when Jeanie Buss peers down below her box through the plexiglass at the spaced-out seats near — but not too near — the AdventHealth Arena court and thinks of where she and the Lakers should be.

She thinks of the season-ticket holders and the security guards and ushers she has known for years from her perch in Staples Center, a space near the home baseline in the first row of the lower bowl where she has held court for years. Some of that has been replicated — the tinny fan noise and "I Love L.A." blaring over the house after wins. But the swell of a real, live crowd enjoying the Lakers' first run to the Finals in a decade cannot be replaced.

From the outer tier of the NBA bubble, where she is staying with close friend Linda Rambis and her brother Joey Buss (both influential team executives), the narrow pane of separation from the game feels bittersweet.

"It feels strange not to be at Staples Center," the Lakers' team owner said in an interview with Southern California News Group, on the eve of Game 5 of the NBA Finals. "Even though I'm here, it still feels like I'm watching it on TV."

But "strange" is a theme of 2020, a year that has plunged Buss, her team and the world into uncertainty, challenges and grief. For much of the NBA restart, Buss hasn't been at the games in person — like many other Lakers fans, she watched from home.

Her viewing party has typically been limited to her and her dog, Delores. Buss is an antsy spectator: She noted that she's powered through her laundry and house-cleaning during games.

"People have asked me why I'm not on the virtual fan board," she laughed. "I can't commit to sitting still for two hours."

Buss, however, is proud of the Lakers, the team that she has presided over with a firmer hand in the last three-and-a-half years since ousting her brother Jim in an effort to end the franchise's longest postseason drought. Even though she had high hopes for these Lakers, they've surpassed her expectations by going 15-4 in the challenging isolation of the bubble. They're just one win away from the organization's 17th NBA championship — which would tie them with the Boston Celtics for the lead among franchises.

It's a far cry from where the Lakers were a year and a half ago. They weathered stormy months last offseason that saw Magic Johnson resign as president of basketball operations then turn on General Manager Rob Pelinka as a reason for his departure. A labored coaching search drew questions about the organization's power structure in the wake of Johnson's exit, and Johnson's public comments drew the wrong kind of attention on the day the Lakers introduced Frank Vogel, the coach they did end up hiring.

A close friend of Johnson and Pelinka, Buss mostly stayed quiet in the public sphere. Internally, she empowered Pelinka to swing a mega-deal for Anthony Davis, then tackle free agency after missing

Through devastating losses and unprecedented challenges, Jeanie Buss helped navigate the Lakers to the 17th championship in franchise history. (AP Images)

out on Kawhi Leonard. While publicly the Lakers faced withering criticism for their start to the long offseason, Buss said she "never wavered" in her support for Pelinka in particular.

"There might have been a lot of conversation in the media or mudslinging on the social media platform," Buss said. "That's not what we're about: We're about the work. Our validation comes from winning."

Now Buss sees the fruits of that labor — a team powered by two superstars in LeBron James and Davis, surrounded by a supporting cast that has been versatile enough to play both big and small depending on the series.

"We pursued the best talent that we could," Buss said. "We were trying to convince Kawhi Leonard to join us, but when he decided, Rob quickly pivoted. As he explained to me, we would be versatile and able to adapt. But you really don't appreciate until you're in the playoffs how well this roster was put together."

As much as the last year has been hard on anyone, it has extracted an emotional toll on Buss. In a month-and-a-half-long span, three hugely influential figures in her life died: her mother, JoAnn Buss, former NBA commissioner David Stern and Kobe Bryant. As she spoke about the losses to SCNG, her voice still cracked with emotion — especially when she mentioned "our beloved Kobe" and his daughter Gianna Bryant.

Her comfort, she said, was Lakers basketball. After Bryant's death, she extracted a small bit of relief from going to games, and the Lakers' lead in the Western Conference standings helped her feel nostalgia for the great seasons of old. And then on March 11, basketball was taken away, too.

Buss said she agreed with Commissioner Adam Silver's decision to immediately suspend the season. She said she can't be sure when basketball will come back to Staples Center, except that the Lakers would "never do anything to jeopardize our fans, players or staff" while complying with all local regulations due to the COVID-19 pandemic.

The hiatus was a time of profound isolation for Buss, but she said she drew (and continues to draw) strength from a number of sources: the inner circle of the Lakers, including Pelinka, Kurt Rambis, Linda Rambis and Joey and Jesse Buss; Phil Jackson, the legendary Lakers coach who continues to offer her guidance after their romantic relationship ended several years ago; Vogel, who Buss said has guided the team with an even hand through a chaotic year.

One of the most powerful voices for her has been James, her franchise player who she has gotten to know more closely since March of 2019, when they finally sat down for a dinner together and James explained his admiration for the Lakers franchise, the work of her father Jerry Buss and her stewardship.

"My relationship with Jeanie I will say is incredible," James said Thursday. "She's an unbelievable owner. She's a powerful woman. I think what she believes in is an extension of her father and continuing to build this legacy of this great franchise."

In a season that has seen the Lakers caught in diplomatic uncertainty in China; devastated by the loss of Bryant; left hanging by the pandemic hiatus and deeply involved in social justice movements, Buss said James' leadership has been like nothing she has ever seen from a basketball player — yes, any of them.

"The strength of LeBron, not only as a basketball player but as a human being has inspired me to be stronger, be more outspoken about things that are wrong in the world today," she said. "I collected comic books growing up, and I would tie a towel around my neck like a cape, like Supergirl or Wonder Woman. LeBron is as close to a real-life superhero as any person I have ever seen."

Buss herself has become more outspoken in recent months regarding social injustices that have become more pronounced since the death of George Floyd in Minneapolis, which she said had a profound influence on her. She and team executive Tim Harris hired Dr. Karida Brown to organize speakers and other seminars for Lakers employees into becoming an anti-racist organization, and the team has worked to donate to Black communities in Los Angeles. The Lakers were part of the movement to make Staples Center into a polling place for the upcoming presidential election.

Personally, Buss has knelt during the national anthem from her box in the bubble in solidarity with her players. On Instagram in June, she shared a letter from a man who addressed her by an epithet for women and wrote: "I now say to hell with the overpaid n—– traitors and the NBA. Go to hell and join (redacted) Kobe Bryant."

Buss said she doesn't usually share such negative sentiments on social media, but she shared this one with a purpose.

"I wanted my white friends to see what hatred is out there and that it is real, and that it does exist, my Black friends are exhausted from carrying this, to have that directed at you, imagine if you had to deal with that every day of your life."

Buss has gotten other similar letters from fans who say they are giving up on the NBA and the Lakers because of its players' stances on social justice issues, race and the league's embrace of such messages.

In one instance, Buss said, she wrote back: She respected the fan's decision to decide not to come or watch the Lakers, but she told him he could always return. The point, she said, is not to tell everyone what to think, but to get them to listen to people with different perspectives and backgrounds.

"I echo what Kareem Abdul-Jabbar has said: We have to educate ourselves, and we have to get to know people who don't look like us," she said. "It's hard and not everyone is going to agree, but I realized what we share is our love of our Laker team. There's our common ground."

What Buss hopes is that soon, Los Angeles will have a reason again to celebrate together. The Finals will end as soon as Friday but no later than Tuesday, and the Lakers are hugely favored to beat the Heat with a 3-1 lead. Buss said she's proud no matter the result.

She'll be watching Game 5 in the booth, behind glass, hoping the NBA can find a means to bring her down to the floor to celebrate the team's first championship in a decade. As the Lakers don their Black Mamba uniforms, she'll be wearing a bracelet inscribed with the numbers 2, 8 and 24 — the jersey numbers of Kobe and Gianna Bryant — and wearing a snake ring gifted by Rambis.

But most of all, she said, she'll be remembering words that Bryant told her that have helped her endure in a difficult year.

"Don't let any setback hold you down," she said. "One day you'll see everything was worth the fight. Everything was worth working hard to achieve." ∎

HEAD COACH

FRANK VOGEL

How Frank Vogel's 'Sabbatical' Year Rejuvenated Him for the Lakers Job

By Kyle Goon | October 18, 2019

It might have been the most valuable film session Shaka Smart took part in all of last season.

Theoretically, Frank Vogel was his guest at the University of Texas, there to watch his practices and study his players and plays. But for five breezy hours in the film room with the then-unemployed head coach, Smart was hard-pressed to say who was learning more as Vogel talked to him about how to disrupt the pick-and-roll attacks of the Longhorns' upcoming opponent.

"The NBA guys, they're ahead of us as college coaches because a higher percentage of their job is basketball," Smart said. "I kind of watch tape when I can on the plane. But sitting with a guy like Frank Vogel, you can pick up so many nuances that really change things at our level."

There's a mental exercise when it comes to finding one's life passion: If you didn't have to work, what would you do? This was no hypothetical for Vogel, who found himself out of an NBA job for the first time in 17 years after the Orlando Magic fired him in April of 2018.

Vogel didn't leap back into a job, but he stayed close to his passion: coaching. The next year was what he calls his "sabbatical" that took him to courts, film rooms and arenas across the country, from Boston to Salt Lake City. It was paradoxically a step back, but also a reminder of why he once hustled his way onto Rick Pitino's Kentucky staff in the first place. And it might just have been the gap year he needed before making his third run as an NBA head coach with the Lakers.

"When I do get in that environment around other coaches, I do have an extra bounce in my step," Vogel said. "There's no wins and losses at stake. I got to just enjoy the game."

Vogel has been in the game for so long, it's easy to forget he's still among the younger tier of current NBA head coaches. Only six are younger than he is. His successor in Indiana, Nate McMillan, is nearly a decade his senior. Vogel never played in the NBA — in fact, the New Jersey native never played Division I college ball. But what he always had was energy and enthusiasm, with a work ethic to match.

David Morway was the general manager of the Indiana Pacers in 2011 when he and team president Larry Bird decided to make Vogel, then just 37, the permanent head coach. Morway is open enough now

On May 20, 2019, Frank Vogel was named head coach of the Lakers. Vogel previously served as head coach of the Indiana Pacers and Orlando Magic. (Daily Breeze: Scott Varley)

o say that "we weren't sure" that it would work out, but with two Eastern Conference finals appearances in the next four seasons, Vogel quickly validated their judgment.

"He was able to gain the group's trust pretty quickly," said Morway, now the assistant general manager for the Utah Jazz. "Frank's really authentic: He is who he is, and that's one of the things I've always truly liked about him. He's just a really good person who also has an excellent basketball mind."

Vogel coached 656 NBA games over the next eight seasons, with a .511 winning percentage, but his tenure in Orlando went south quickly. With a young core, the Magic lost games, and the front office that hired Vogel was quickly swept out after just a year. When Vogel was fired, he had just finished a grinder of a decade.

Instead of forcing his way back onto an NBA bench, Vogel decided to stay in Orlando for another year, where his young daughters were going to school. And then he started making some calls.

Central Florida coach Johnny Dawkins had spent the previous two years watching Vogel from across town in Orlando, and even attended a Magic practice. As he worked on coaching the 7-foot-6 Tacko Fall last season, he welcomed any chance he could to get input from Vogel, whose best Indiana teams were anchored by 7-2 Roy Hibbert. Dawkins said, as he hoped, Vogel was helpful in dropping a few tips.

"When you think of what he did there, he put guys where they can be successful," Dawkins said. "He was a force there because Frank allowed Roy Hibbert to play to his strengths."

Other college coaches who had spent time admiring Vogel's work, especially his defenses, from afar were surprised when Vogel reached out to them. Smart had never met Vogel before, for example, but had appreciated the connection Vogel seemed to have with his players and the intensity he could drive — something Smart has firsthand experience with sculpting his own defenses.

Although Vogel arrived, on the surface, to examine the Longhorns' practices and culture, Smart found himself writing down plenty of notes, too. But he also found Vogel to be receptive.

"He naturally has a humility about him," he said. "And I think with his knowledge, it can go really, really well to have those two traits together."

It's more difficult to pry intimate details of his visits with NBA teams, but Vogel visited several of them. He spent three days with the Jazz, getting access to coaches' meetings. He similarly got to sit in on multiple staff meetings with the Boston Celtics, where he was able to see how one of his coaching friends, Brad Stevens, runs things. He visited with Brett Brown in Philadelphia, Rick Carlisle in Dallas and Billy Donovan in Oklahoma City.

Vogel called the extensive tour eye-opening. Every coach tries to add new facets to their program every season, but Vogel estimated that "80 to 90 percent" stays the same, simply because working coaches rarely get to see what other staffs are doing.

"To be able to step away and be a part of these other camps for a few days each time, you get to see a completely different way of doing things," he said. "Whether it's drill work, how staff meetings are run, or how the practices are run, how much delegation is going on, the terminology of defensive systems, and your offensive rules for running the break. There's really an endless list of things you observe when you're seeing another person's program that you will never see if you don't get that opportunity."

Among Vogel's other takeaways was how to loosen up the grind of an NBA season: Stevens would occasionally break out a game of dodgeball or other activities to lighten the atmosphere. Brown is famous for having his players deliver PowerPoint presentations about non-basketball topics, and Vogel said the way the 76ers were able to open up internal dialogue was enlightening.

Said Vogel, who incidentally had the Lakers throw footballs while warming up in a nearby park earlier this week: "There is a time to have fun while you're grinding."

The teams Vogel visited with enjoyed his sense of energy and enthusiasm. They welcomed his insights as they game-planned or practiced. Jazz coach Quin Snyder, who didn't know Vogel well before his trip to Utah, wound up giving him more access than he originally envisioned.

"Clearly when Frank came in, he just has a great attitude," said Morway, who helped arrange the visit. "Obviously Quin was comfortable and enjoyed having his willingness and eagerness to share ideas. Frank's passion for the game — it comes across."

That energy was part of the reason the Lakers, after flirtations with Ty Lue and Monty Williams early in their coaching search, decided Vogel was a good candidate to take over. Another was his aptitude for collaboration: The team wanted a lot of experience around him, including former head coaches Jason Kidd and Lionel Hollins, and went on to hire Phil Handy, who has been to the last five Finals with Cleveland and Toronto.

"Knowing that the level of roster we were building was full of guys with high, high basketball IQs, the more basketball minds we could have as part of the staff, we felt better," Lakers general manager Rob Pelinka said. "And Frank loved that vision."

The coaches Vogel visited with over the past year believe the Lakers will reflect their head coach: organized, hard-working and passionate. While some basketball pundits already have gossiped as to whether Vogel will last in Los Angeles, which is undoubtedly a more high-pressure job than he's had before, those who

know Vogel have confidence that he'll find his way.

After Vogel was hired and the Lakers traded for Anthony Davis, Kentucky coach John Calipari — who he visited last year — chatted with him about what the offense might look like with the former Wildcat as its centerpiece. Calipari liked what he heard, thinking that it sounded similar to how Davis played at Kentucky, on the way to becoming a national champion and national player of the year.

Among coaches he's known, Calipari compared some of Vogel's traits to Larry Brown and Jay Wright.

"There's that one thing about following the herd, then there's the guy who's not afraid to step out and try different things," Calipari said. "This stuff is hard, what we do. For a guy to step out and try something new and not gonna go down an easy path, those are the guys who really do special things."

The preseason has gone relatively smoothly for the Lakers, at least on the coaching side. Vogel said he's tried to shorten practices compared to what he used to do for his younger Pacers teams. But he's also thrown more concepts at them faster than he usually would.

Whatever happens with Vogel's Lakers' tenure, he's confident about one thing — he's spent enough time studying what works.

"You don't ever really wanna be let go from a job, but like anything that happens in life, you gotta make the best of your situation," he said. "It really was a great experience for me last year." ∎

THE LONG ROAD BACK

Lakers' Rajon Rondo, Dwight Howard Relish Return to Finals

By Kyle Goon | September 29, 2020

For Lakers fans, a return to the Finals for the first time in a decade is a reason to look back on a triumphant past. But reminiscing isn't so fun for everyone in the locker room.

It's also the first time Rajon Rondo has been back to the Finals since 2010. Back then, he was on the Boston Celtics team that fell under the crushing wheel of Kobe Bryant, Pau Gasol and the Lakers after taking a 3-2 lead.

"I think I blurred a lot of it out: It was ugly." Rondo deadpanned Tuesday, as he took the stage ahead of the Lakers' series with the Miami Heat. "But that's a long, long time ago, and I look forward to obviously changing the chapter and continuing to go past this different chapter in my life and write a better story ending."

When it comes to chapters in the Finals, there's been a long gap for two of the team's key veterans off the bench: Rondo (10 years) and Dwight Howard (11 years). In both cases, their last Finals-contending team was bested by the Lakers and Bryant.

While they've both been Lakers for more than a year now, there was at least a dose of surrealism that they're both now wearing the jerseys of their once-sworn foes. It paired well with an already strange scene: A Finals media day held in the NBA bubble at Disney World, huge crowds of media replaced by two-dozen-odd reporters and Zoom stations.

Ironically, Howard remembered, the critique of his best Orlando Magic teams was snide comments that they were a secondary concern to getting time in the local theme parks. Getting to the Finals in 2009 helped change some perceptions, he said.

"People just thought that, 'Hey, we're playing the Magic. We can go to Disney World, Universal Studios the night before the game and we don't have too much to worry about because it's just the Magic,'" he said. "Then into a team that's like, 'Man, when you go against the Magic, you got to be ready.'"

While the gap between Finals berths is, in one sense, a credit to how long Rondo's and Howard's careers have lasted, it's also a reminder of how early they first experienced success. Rondo was 21 when he won a title in Boston in 2008, just his second year in the league. Howard was 23 when his Magic were beaten in five games by the Lakers in 2009.

Rondo went to the Finals twice in his first four seasons and has been searching for a way back ever since. He's tried to impart on younger players how important it is to take advantage of these rare opportunities.

"It's a completely different experience, and understanding that this doesn't come often or annually," he said. "Being back here over a decade later is a very humbling experience, and I'm letting my young guys know from all the rookies to the second or third-year players like (Kyle Kuzma), that this

Rajon Rondo goes to the basket against the Oklahoma City Thunder as teammate Dwight Howard looks on. Veterans Rondo and Howard, who burst onto the NBA scene more than a decade ago, played key roles for the 2019-20 Lakers. (AP Images)

opportunity doesn't come often. Guys search for this moment their entire career, and we definitely have to seize the moment."

Howard is burdened by even more history than Rondo: He's yet to win a championship in a career many deem worthy of the Hall of Fame. His first stint with the Lakers was heralded with championship expectations but ended with a whimper and a first-round sweep, the start of a frustrating stretch in the prime of his career where he couldn't advance back to the Finals.

Coming back and winning with the Lakers has been cathartic: Howard said the Saturday night when the Lakers won the Western Conference Finals was a celebration filled with emotion. But he tried to remind himself that the larger prize was still ahead.

"I sit at home, sit in the room, and I walk around the bubble and I just think about how that feeling would be just to hold up that trophy," he said. "It brings me to tears every time I think about it." ■

CARRY THAT WEIGHT

LeBron James Has Helped Anthony Davis Shoulder the Lakers' Pressure to Win

By Kyle Goon | September 17, 2020

In the middle of the Lakers' biggest win so far this postseason, Anthony Davis was struggling. It was hard to tell from the 6-foot-10 forward's body language that his team was blowing out the Houston Rockets in Game 5. He hung his head. He slumped his shoulders. As he shuffled to the bench during a timeout in the third quarter, he brushed past several open palms of his teammates, who looked at him with concern.

Davis was in the midst of what would be a 4-for-9 night from the field with six turnovers, a frustrating slog that took him nearly a half to score a basket at all. Even when ahead, the 27-year-old has a way of letting tough games get to him.

"When I'm playing, I'm a perfectionist," Davis told Southern California News Group. "I want to make every shot, make every play defensively, I want to be in the right spots. That game, I just wasn't … I just happened to be bleeding."

Even from the bench, LeBron James can take in the entire court with his vision. And as Davis looked over to the sideline, James shouted his way: "Just take a deep breath! Just breathe!"

It's simple advice, but coming from James — Davis' partner and mentor in this long and unthinkably challenging season — it means the world. It took some time, but Davis stiffened up and played out the close out, in which the Lakers would smash the Rockets by 23 points.

There's been plenty of moments this season when James, who has had times in his career when he's been tough on his teammates, can sense that Davis needs to be picked up.

"It's a guy who strives for perfection and wants to be great — I know," he told SCNG of that moment. "Anytime you see someone like that may be getting down on themselves or feel like they can be so much better, it's great to just, you know, breathe. Just breathe, take a deep breath, center yourself and get back to work."

The NBA bubble has been a strange environment for pressure, which has been refracted and intensified in unpredictable ways. It's cleared the path for culture- and chemistry-driven teams like the Denver Nuggets and the Miami Heat, and has callously crushed once-favored contenders Milwaukee and the Clippers replete with star talent.

Davis has gotten a feel for that pressure, too, and person he's looked to the most in those moments is James, a three-time champion in the mold of the competitor that Davis strives to be.

It's not always a reminder to breathe (it would be naive to ignore here that James is a spokesman for a meditation app). But sometimes it's lighthearted banter. When Davis checks out at the end of the third quarter and James checks in with a lead, Davis often tells him: "Alright now, I'm not trying to play in the fourth."

I've got your back, James said.

"So, just little things like that where we can encourage each other, just help each other out during the season, because it can get tough," Davis said. "You got two guys who guys look up to and look to lean on, and it can get tough especially for a whole season. Luckily it's two guys and not one."

Davis was a solo act for much of his time in New Orleans, and while he produced statistically, he struggled with other aspects of stardom. Fans prodded

LeBron James (left) played dual roles as both partner and mentor for Anthony Davis during the pair's first season together as Lakers teammates. (AP Images)

and picked at his injury history, which were widely seen at the time as minor ailments. Davis went to the playoffs just twice, and his only truly brilliant run with the Pelicans was to sweep Portland in 2018.

Even though he had Rajon Rondo and Jrue Holiday as teammates during that run, and he seemed to thrive when DeMarcus Cousins arrived via trade, Davis found it difficult to elevate the franchise when it fell mostly on his shoulders. Through seven years, Davis had made three All-NBA teams, but what he wanted most — a championship — seemed devastatingly out of reach: "We know what the bigger goal is, especially for me."

While Davis has a 7-foot-5 wingspan and athleticism that made him one of the most fluid and productive big men in the NBA, he needed guidance in how to win. And he finally has that in James.

One of the most striking things Paul George said when the Clippers blew their 3-1 lead to the Nuggets was that it was the first time he had "not been considered an underdog." Expectations to win are difficult to shoulder, and in James' view: "Some people was built for this moment and some people were not."

Davis has handled that before as a marquee player at Kentucky, which had a blue blood culture and star recruits. Davis has felt his Lakers tenure has had a similar feel. And no one has more playoff experience to draw on than James, who during the last series claimed the most individual playoff wins in NBA history. With a 3-6 record in the Finals, he's felt the weight of title contender disappointment, and many times come back from it.

"Obviously any team LeBron's on is more than likely gonna be favored, and he's kinda helped me with that," he said. "It's gonna be 'pressure,' but you gotta want that and embrace it. And that's all I've been doing, embracing that and just being able to go out there and just play."

There's been signs that James has responded to Davis' presence, too. While Davis has little to teach the 35-year-old about playoff series, James' re-embrace of

defense in his 17th year has been staggering because it has been some time since he played this well on that side of the ball. James' last Cleveland team that went to the Finals had a 112.1 defensive rating when he was on the court; in his Lakers' minutes during the regular season, the team has had a 103.6 defensive rating.

James is not one to admit that he ever draws motivation from others — "I'm an only child so I had to push myself," he said — but he did acknowledge that he understands he has to play hard when Davis is looking to him as an example.

"In the sense of being older than AD, I think it's showing him how much I put into my craft, and hopefully it trickles down to him," James said in his Thursday press conference. "I feel like I would be cheating him if he came to be a part of this and I was cheating the game in some way, shape or form. It's not an example I would ever set for any of my teammates, not just AD, but anybody I ever played with."

James is famously tight-fisted when it comes to trusting teammates, and his style has grated with many of them. Complicated relationships with teammates like Chris Bosh and Kevin Love worked themselves out, aided by the final prize. Relationships like his with Kyrie Irving deteriorated over time, even though they won a championship together.

Maybe what James has already seen so far has helped him be the kind voice to Davis rather than the harsh, demanding one. Davis has averaged 27.6 points (more than James) with 10.9 rebounds and 4.1 assists. He's guarded every position at least once, and he didn't hesitate when the Lakers moved him to full-time center against the Rockets. His defensive presence has helped the Lakers extinguish some of the best scorers in the league.

James sees it: Davis has the talent. He just needs the occasional reminder to breathe, then play.

"I feel like it was just my opportunity to say something," James told SCNG. "But he's special. He's very special." ∎

In their first season as teammates, LeBron James and Anthony Davis led the Lakers through unprecedented obstacles en route to the franchise's 17th championship. (AP Images)

ROAD TO THE FINALS

Los Angeles Lakers and Denver Nuggets players and coaches kneel on the sideline during the national anthem prior to Game 1 of the Western Conference Finals. After the NBA season resumed in Florida in July, several of the league's players, coaches, and executives used their platforms to advocate for social justice. (AP Images)

WESTERN CONFERENCE QUARTERFINALS GAME 1

AUGUST 18, 2020 | LAKE BUENA VISTA, FLORIDA

TRAIL BLAZERS 100, LAKERS 93

OUT OF SYNC

Lakers Stunned by Damian Lillard and the Trail Blazers' Fourth-Quarter Rally

By Kyle Goon

There's a saying that time is undefeated. In the NBA bubble, Dame Time is 8-2.

For days, the Lakers have said they don't face a regular first-round matchup in these playoffs, and Game 1 showed they were right. Damian Lillard, the hot-shooting Portland star who has scored more points than anyone else this summer, fired a fourth-quarter 3-point shot a step shy of the halfcourt with just over three minutes to go — the key three of his 34 points.

It lit an 11-4 final rally that gave Portland, the supposed eight seed, a 100-93 victory over the Lakers and a lot to think about before the teams meet again Thursday.

"We didn't take care of business," the Lakers' LeBron James. "But we got another opportunity on Thursday to even the series, and that's my only mindset."

Portland overcame a Herculian effort by James, who scored 23 points and grabbed 17 rebounds and 16 assists — the only player to ever carve out that particular stat line in playoff history of all three categories over 15. Anthony Davis had 28 points, but as a team, the Lakers looked entirely out of sync offensively, shooting 35 percent from the floor and just 5 for 32 on 3-pointers.

The Lakers continued to assert that they believe in their shooting, which has not been thawed by the Florida heat, with coach Frank Vogel saying that eventually the law of averages will even them out. But while the Trail Blazers didn't shoot particularly well against an aggressive Lakers defense, their late-game execution spoke to the polish of playing for their playoff lives for the last three weeks.

"(LeBron) would've had over 20 assists if we knocked down threes at the rate that we're capable of and at the rate we will," Vogel said. "Yeah, it's certainly disappointing to lose this game, and always obviously with the performance he had. He was spectacular."

The last stretch was key. After James and Davis missed four straight free throws, Danny Green hit a game-tying lay-up at 89-all. But Lillard ambushed the Lakers defense with his near-halfcourt bomb, a blow that seemed to stun them for the next few possessions as Carmelo Anthony and Gary Trent Jr. hit 3-pointers on the open backside. The Lakers would go on to say these mistakes were correctable — but in the moment, they were devastating.

After a fourth-quarter 3-pointer, Lillard ran back to the other end of the court and danced as "Blow the Whistle" by fellow Oakland native Too Short blasted over the AdventHealth Arena speakers.

"If you're in a rhythm like that, confident player," Kyle Kuzma said, "(expletive), I'd do the same. Tip my hat to him."

Adding to the Lakers' early woes were whistles. They gave up 27 first-half free throws, as three Lakers got at least three fouls before halftime (and Dwight Howard got four). There was another unexpected interruption halfway through the second quarter: An official determined the rim needed straightening, and a game crew member spent several minutes cranking the hoop into its proper position.

Maybe that's what did it for the Lakers, who finally started hitting 3-pointers and closed the gap

LeBron James lies on the court after committing a foul during the second half of Game 1. Despite James' historic line of 23 points, 17 rebounds and 16 assists, the Lakers fell to the Portland Trail Blazers, 100-93. (AP Images)

from 16 points to nothing, taking a lead on a Davis dunk assisted by James. James' urgency helped power the Lakers on both ends to a 31-21 advantage in the quarter, and he had 10 assists by intermission.

"The team is really good when we were running," Davis said. "As long as we're playing with pace, it's tough to beat us. It's when we slow down and not running that we're in trouble."

The Lakers did have at least one positive experience with officiating. Vogel successfully challenged a collision between James and Hassan Whiteside early in the fourth quarter that not only kept the Blazers from taking the lead, but gave Whiteside his fourth foul. But it was not enough to overcome defensive miscues that ended up costing the game.

"We were slow on the rotation," James said. "So that's things we can control."

The last Lakers playoff game was 2,670 days ago, a forgettable loss to the San Antonio Spurs in a first-round sweep. Their last win was on May 18, 2012, a

lone second-round series win over a feisty Oklahoma City team that would go on to lose to James' then-Miami Heat team for his first championship win. It was the organization's first playoff game without Kobe Bryant on the roster in 24 years — and the initials of their lost superstar were stitched to their gold jerseys, not far from their hearts.

But again, James lamented that there were no fans to play for. Perhaps it is upsetting the natural order of the NBA: In the East, the top-seeded Milwaukee Bucks also lost their Game 1 against the eight-seed Orlando Magic — and theirs was not particularly close. It was the first time in NBA history that both No. 1 seeds had lost their first game in the first round.

Portland continued to float on its dream as a team of destiny, shouting in the corner near their bench, "Three more!" as they walked off the court.

The Lakers will have to wait at least two more days for another franchise playoff victory — one that doesn't look like it will come easily. ∎

WESTERN CONFERENCE QUARTERFINALS GAME 2

AUGUST 20, 2020 | LAKE BUENA VISTA, FLORIDA

LAKERS 111, TRAIL BLAZERS 88

ATTACKING THE RIM

Damian Lillard Injured as Lakers Punish Trail Blazers in Game 2

By Kyle Goon

After a disappointing Game 1, LeBron James gave his co-star some space. Anthony Davis hadn't looked himself in his Lakers playoff debut, too often settling for jumpers and, by his own self-critique, slow and hesitant on rotations. But after giving Davis time to digest the 0-1 lead the Lakers had ceded to the Portland Trail Blazers, James said the very thing Davis needed to hear: Everything would be OK. Davis. The series. The mission.

"He kind of was there to encourage me and keep me level-headed, because it was just one game," Davis said. "But our relationship has been great this entire season. I've kind of just been leaning on him this entire season to figure out the tricks and trades of playing with a guy like him and a team like this."

What Davis seemed to realize, and what the Lakers seemed to finally realize Thursday night is that they do have an advantage on their No. 8-seed opponent: They can push them around when they choose.

The one-time bullies of the Western Conference — who twice beat these Trail Blazers in their own gym in December — rediscovered their front-runner mentality with muscular drives to the rim, with urgent strides up and down the court; with 3-pointers and dunks splashing more generously than two nights before, and with rebounds taken right from their opponents' fingers.

With so many things about these playoffs spun completely topsy-turvy, some normalcy found its way onto the court at last for the Lakers, who completely blew out Portland 111-88. Bench players were allowed to scrimmage for the entire fourth quarter — the Lakers led by as much as 33 points, tying the series at one game apiece and giving the streaking Blazers the smarting feeling of a loss.

Davis was the most transformed, from a meek, midrange shooter in Game 1 to a relentless two-way aggressor in Game 2. While he only scored three more points (31), he made five more shots on three fewer attempts in just three quarters, driving in against a largely helpless Wenyen Gabriel and Jusuf Nurkic to push inside for his points. On the other end, Davis helped on Portland's red-hot shooters — helping hold Damian Lillard and C.J. McCollum to just 12 of 30 shooting from the floor.

Davis used the words "desperation" and "urgency" — the first time the Lakers have showed those things on the court since March, before the hiatus.

The night was over for the Blazers in the third quarter, when Davis finally found his shooting touch, scoring eight straight points including a pair of 3-pointers to push the lead to insurmountable.

The Trail Blazers were also forced to disengage late in the third when Lillard, the offensive superhero of the bubble, walked off court wincing after dislocating his left index finger. An X-ray came back negative for

JaVale McGee dunks during the third quarter. McGee scored 10 points and grabbed eight rebounds in the Lakers' Game 2 win. (AP Images)

fractures, but it's a major concern for a Blazers team that is already injured and has spent three weeks punching above its weight.

The Blazers have not scored fewer than 93 points all year, but they couldn't find daylight to shoot through against the Lakers.

"We want to take away their confidence as early as possible, because they can get going very quickly," Davis said. "If they come in to shoot, it's gonna be a tough shot with a hand in your face."

Portland anticipated a rally by the Lakers, who fell in Game 1 in their first playoff appearance in seven years. They responded by putting pressure on James, who labored for his 10 points and seven assists, coughing up six turnovers in the process.

But the supporting cast came alive like Davis himself. The Lakers' shooters partly redeemed themselves for an abysmal Game 1 performance, and no one more than Kentavious Caldwell-Pope, who made 5 for 8 (and 4 for 6 on 3-pointers). He was 0 for 9 in Game 1.

"I shot the ball terribly, I wouldn't even say 'bad,'" Caldwell-Pope said. "Just tried to forget about that and not try to carry it to Game 2. Have my mind clear and be ready to play. … I'm a shooter, and shooters shoot."

Even when the Lakers' threes weren't falling, they made up for it by attacking the rim and the glass. The Lakers had 14 offensive rebounds thanks to an emphasis cleaning up the boards, led by Davis (11) and JaVale McGee (8). The Lakers finished with 20 second chance points and outscored the Blazers by 12 in the paint.

Game 3 tips off on Saturday at 5:30 p.m. PDT. And the Lakers expect themselves to carry the same energy into that one.

"We don't view it as an underdog matchup: They're a heavyweight with the way they play and with a player like Dame Lillard," Coach Frank Vogel said. "We're gonna have to battle the way we did tonight every game of the series." ■

The Lakers' relentless defense held the Trail Blazers to just 40 percent shooting from the field in Game 2. (AP Images)

WESTERN CONFERENCE QUARTERFINALS GAME 3

AUGUST 22, 2020 | LAKE BUENA VISTA, FLORIDA

LAKERS 116, TRAIL BLAZERS 108

IN THE DRIVER'S SEAT

LeBron James scores 38 as Lakers Take 2-1 Series Lead

By Kyle Goon

As LeBron James flew past him for his last driving lay-up of the game, Jusuf Nurkic cast his eyes down and exhaled deeply.

The question for a week had been if the Lakers felt the urgency the Trail Blazers have been living since they arrived in the bubble. As the Lakers headed back to the bench with a double-digit lead into a timeout, looking pert and confident, the axis of that particular narrative seemed to finally tilt their way.

The Western Conference 1 seed beat up against on Portland, the plucky underdog of the last few weeks which finally seemed to lose its steam in a 116-106 Lakers win.

LeBron James was his most assertive scoring self with 38 points, the most he's scored in the bubble. Anthony Davis had 29 points, turning on a sometimes mercurial top gear in the second half. And the Blazers seemed to hit a wall — in opening up a series advantage, the Lakers illustrated how hard it will be to catch them.

"Just trying to wear them down," Davis said. "Obviously they've been playing a lot. Since they've been here, they've been playing like Game 7s. So it's our job to kind of keep putting the pressure on them and keep running as the bigs, and that's what we're gonna do."

Playing with a splint on his left finger, Damian Lillard still scored 34 points, and CJ McCollum scored 28. But the supporting cast was blown away trying to keep up with the Lakers, whose 40-point third quarter helped swing momentum. Overwhelmed Nurkic and Hassan Whiteside combined for just 18 points and 15 rebounds, while the Blazers bench scored only eight points.

After summoning "urgency" and "desperation" in their Game 2 blowout, the Lakers started the game with neither of those things. A trudging pace combined with an abysmal start at the free throw line — missing 10 of their first 20 — gave Portland a narrow lead for much of the first half.

The dynamic only began to change as James took a more aggressive scoring role, whirling into the paint through contact to finish off the glass. It was a side of James that has been rarely seen so far in the restart: In Game 1, he chose distributor rather than bucket-getter, racking up 16 assists. But studying tape of the first two games, he said, made him see that more assertiveness was required.

"Every game calls for a different situation," he said. "Tonight, I just wanted to try to be aggressive and see if I can get into the paint, see if I can find my guys and I was able to do that early."

James drive seemed to filter down, particularly to Davis who shot just three times in the first half. He scored 23 in the second half, and on the glass, he and James combined for 23 of the Lakers 55 rebounds, for a plus-17 margin over their opponents.

The Lakers shot 6 for 12 from 3-point range in the third, especially getting a boost from Kentavious Caldwell-Pope (13 points), who started the game cold. It helped them weather a vintage rally from Carmelo

LeBron James scored 38 points to lead the Lakers in Game 3. (AP Images)

Anthony, who scored 13 of his points in the third quarter including a stretch with three straight baskets.

Alex Caruso played one of the biggest roles as the Lakers' back-up ball-handler, helping build leads with Davis in key stretches while James rested on the bench. He finished with 7 assists, the most competent backup point guard the Lakers have had since Rajon Rondo fractured his thumb last month (he missed Game 3 with pregame back spasms). Caruso also took on the task of guarding Lillard and McCollum late. In one fourth-quarter possession, he single-handedly closed out on Lillard on one wing to Lillard on the other.

Caruso finished with a plus-10 rating. It helped, he said, to be passing to Davis.

"For the most part, we just ran a simple high ball screen, and we did a good job manipulating the defense," he said. "And then I just got to him on time and on target, and he did the rest, to be honest."

The game seemed closed in the fourth quarter as James threw back-to-back lobs to Dwight Howard and Davis, which Nurkic and Whiteside seemed helpless to stop. Davis also found his midrange touch again late, stepping out for jumpers off of Caruso's pick-and-pop direction.

James moved to 158 playoff wins in his career, passing Hall of Famer and frequent opponent Tim Duncan whom he met in three Finals: "Basically, he lived in the postseason. That was his address. So, for me to be linked with a great in the Big Fundamental, it means a lot."

With just three more playoff wins, he'll tie Derek Fisher for the most ever.

After the Spurs topped James back in 2007, Duncan told James, "This is going to be your league in a little while." Saturday, James gave a strong case that 13 years later, it still might be. ■

WESTERN CONFERENCE QUARTERFINALS GAME 4

WESTERN CONFERENCE QUARTERFINALS GAME 4

AUGUST 24, 2020 | LAKE BUENA VISTA, FLORIDA

LAKERS 135, TRAIL BLAZERS 115

MAMBA MENTALITY

On Mamba Night, Lakers Make Short Work of Trail Blazers

By Kyle Goon

Back in January when the Lakers and Portland Trail Blazers would meet for the last time in the regular season, the Lakers were a wreck. They had tears in their eyes and weights on their chests.

They were missing Kobe Bryant, the mentor, the family man, the poster on some of their walls who had represented winning, passion and dedication.

Nearly seven months later on Monday night, with a playoff game to win, the Lakers didn't mourn. They celebrated the Kobe who would have taken the court if he could've for this Game 4 against the Trail Blazers: the Black Mamba.

With a sense of ruthless urgency, the Lakers swiftly stomped on their eighth-seeded opponent, scoring 43 points in the first quarter and never letting up in a 135-115 blowout win to take a 3-1 series lead. LeBron James played another starring role, scoring 30 points and adding 10 assists in the third straight victory for the Lakers since a postseason-opening defeat.

Universally, they said afterward, they wanted to win this one for Kobe.

"We know they're coming out with a sense of desperation, and we wanted to be the harder playing team with that sense of urgency we need on both ends of the floor," Anthony Davis said. "Realizing that the first time we played again after the tragedy was also against Portland, and they were able to take that one from us at home. But we wanted to make sure we did everything we could to get this win for him."

The Lakers took a 16-point lead before the Blazers scored once, with Davis leading the charge on both ends by smothering the Portland scorers and ripping off the nets with his shooting. His slow starting ritual of past games was forgotten, as the Lakers had a 20-point lead in just 10 minutes.

Portland couldn't stop Davis, but in the third quarter, back spasms did (he said after the game he would be fine for Game 5). He checked out early with 18 points, five assists, five rebounds and two blocks in just 17-and-a-half minutes of work. The Lakers outscored the Blazers by 37 in those minutes.

Lakers coach Frank Vogel said he was awed by Davis' dominance, including a sequence where he notched two deflections and dove for a loose ball

"He was just all over the place on the defensive end, and then he was just making everything," said Vogel, who added that he had never seen anything like it.

Even after the Lakers subbed out Davis, one star was enough — thanks in no small part to perimeter shooting that came alive to finish with 17 threes. James had four of them, just one fewer than Kyle Kuzma who finished with 18 points.

The game had potentially devastating news for the Blazers, who lost Damian Lillard in the third quarter to a right knee injury. Yahoo Sports reported the Portland guard, who led the bubble in scoring during seeding games, was undergoing an MRI.

Portland was led by Jusuf Nurkic, who scored 20 points.

The Lakers ran enough laps around the Blazers to start showing off. Late in the second quarter, James pulled up a step shy of the halfcourt logo to drill a long three — the range where Lillard has created his aura

Alex Caruso passes past the reach of Portland's Gary Trent Jr. during the second quarter. Wearing Black Mamba jerseys to honor the late Kobe Bryant, the Lakers topped the Trail Blazers 135-115 in Game 4 to take a 3-1 series lead. (AP Images)

as one of the league's most dangerous shooters. As he skipped back on defense, he took exaggerated nods of his head in triumphant celebration, a gesture Bryant might have made after sinking such a shot.

James said he had trouble at times focusing before the game because of the news of the shooting of Jacob Blake, a man in Wisconsin shot seven times by police, who had been the subject of a viral video. James lamented that another unarmed man had been shot by police a day before the Lakers wanted to celebrate Bryant and have a huge day in their organization.

"And I said I have a job to do, because I'm here, because I committed," he said. "And when I commit to something, I feel like I have to come through on it, because that's just who I am. But that does not mean that I don't see what's going on and I won't say anything."

While the Lakers' Black Mamba jerseys were decked with the snake scale texture of Bryant's scoring assassin persona, there was at least one small crack in the armor: On the right shoulder of each jersey was a heart-shaped patch with No. 2, the number of Gianna Bryant.

Bryant's spirit seemed threaded into the game in inexplicable ways, too. During one stirring moment after Kentavious Caldwell-Pope hit a contested lay-up, the scoreboard briefly reflected the Lakers' 24-8 lead — Bryant's two jersey numbers.

"When I looked up there and saw 24 and 8, I said, 'OK, he's here in the building,'" James said. "So it's a beautiful night for our franchise, and something I'll always remember from this moment in the playoffs." ∎

WESTERN CONFERENCE QUARTERFINALS GAME 5

AUGUST 29, 2020 | LAKE BUENA VISTA, FLORIDA

LAKERS 131, TRAIL BLAZERS 122

RISE UP

LeBron James, Anthony Davis Dazzle as Lakers Top Trail Blazers in First-Round Series

By Kyle Goon

It took three days longer to close the series than the Lakers expected, and for three-and-a-half quarters, the Trail Blazers kept hope alive that it would take more.

But that very faint flame was extinguished by a cruising Anthony Davis, driving into a clear lane in transition on the other end of a LeBron James bounce pass late in the fourth quarter. Before the series started, Portland's chief challenge was to stop him. They never were able to.

So the Lakers advanced, but not without effort. A 131-122 Game 5 victory didn't inspire the kind of confidence a championship contender should. But days after acknowledging that closeout games are the hardest to win, James didn't let the Lakers miss the opportunity: He scored 36 points in a triple-double, and helped feed Davis' 43.

The superstar duo bested the Trail Blazers who had only one half their pair. James and Davis combined to go for 28 for 37 from the field.

It happened after tense days of off-court drama following the protest of the Milwaukee Bucks on Wednesday, hours before the Lakers were supposed to tip this Game 5. James acknowledged he was frustrated in the immediate aftermath of the strike that he had been thrust into a situation without a long-term plan. Of leaving the bubble, he admitted, "It probably crossed my mind, sure," but claimed it wasn't because of the strike.

"From a fan's perspective and from a basketball junkie, it's the best thing that you could ever ask for, basketball games over and over and over and over and over," he said. "When you're trying to create change, you can't lose sight of what the main thing is and why we came out here."

But he took care of business off the court, becoming a key figure in the player-driven effort to get owners to turn arenas into voting sites and form a social justice coalition. Then Saturday, he took care of business on it.

The Lakers clinched their first playoff series win since 2012, in a first-round bout with the Denver Nuggets. In the gulf between lies the worst stretch in franchise history, including six years without any postseason at all. But topping the Blazers was a needed first step in starting to restore some shine to the Lakers organization after those days in the wilderness — and bring them a step closer to its first title since 2010. Their second round opponent will be either the Houston Rockets or Oklahoma City Thunder (Houston has a 3-2 lead).

But for much of the slog-fest on Monday night, the Lakers hardly looked like a team worthy of those ambitions. It was the only game of the series that the Lakers didn't have to deal with Damian Lillard, who left the bubble in the last week after suffering a right knee sprain in Game 4. But the Blazers, undeterred, donned black head bands as they faced their

Kyle Kuzma shoots over Portland's Hassan Whiteside during the first half of Game 5. (AP Images)

elimination, and played with a sense of desperation that the Lakers had predicted but not prepared for.

C.J. McCollum was persistent enough for two, both charging into the paint and knocking down jumpers. The Lakers' defensive scheme that had contained the best of him seemed broken down and possibly the best player in the West to never be an All-Star rained down 36 points in response.

He found a rejuvenated Carmelo Anthony as a willing backcourt mate: He had 27 points, finding particular relish in match-ups with James, his fellow 2003 draft partner and close friend.

"They didn't get this far to just give up. And we knew that," Davis said. "And closeout games are already tough. But just tried to keep fighting."

Days of contention and negotiation during league-wide protest were restorative to the players' messages of social justice, but were also exhausting. Both the Lakers and Trail Blazers had players at the forefront of the NBPA in discussions to advance certain social justice causes, and both Danny Green and McCollum spoke on Friday of getting little to no sleep. Coaches had attempted to keep scheming simple — Frank Vogel said in his practices for Game 5, he merely wanted to give his players a chance to run up and down the floor.

The lag in focus was especially apparent as the teams took more than four minutes in real time to play out the final 1.1 seconds of the first quarter — J.R. Smith accidentally caused a turnover by taking an inbounds pass while he was out of bounds.

That seemed to change at the start of the third quarter, as Davis and Kentavious Caldwell-Pope stepped up, helping rip off a 13-0 run to gain a modest separation from their short-handed opponents. It was in this period that Davis found the most assertive version of himself that helped turn the series after a 0-1 start: He ripped a rebound out of Mario Hezonja's hands underneath the basket before rising up for a slam.

As the Lakers left the court with the win, James seemed to finally unbutton from his drama-filled week. He went over to Anthony, who he now boasts a 8-2 record against in playoff games, and gave him a hug and a few words. Then he waited for Davis near the corner of the arena, salsa dancing to "Smooth Operator" before shuffling out the door.

"That's what you do when you close out a series," James said to a laughing Davis. "You let that (expletive) out now." ∎

LeBron James finished Game 5 with a triple double, scoring 36 points to go along with 10 rebounds and 10 assists as the Lakers clinched their first playoff series win since 2012. (AP Images)

WESTERN CONFERENCE SEMIFINALS GAME 1

SEPTEMBER 4, 2020 | LAKE BUENA VISTA, FLORIDA

ROCKETS 112, LAKERS 97

NO EXCUSES

Lakers Fail to Match the Energy, Speed of Revved Up Rockets in Game 1

By Kyle Goon

So much for fatigue. So much for playing tiny lineups. So much for an entire organization feeling crushing pressure to advance.

The Lakers won the tip-off against the small-ball Houston Rockets in Game 1 of their second-round series Friday, and then every perceived advantage they had entering the night vanished.

The Rockets had sharper stars, with James Harden and Russell Westbrook primed and scoring 60 points combined to 45 from LeBron James and Anthony Davis. The Rockets had a more cohesive defense, which forced the Lakers to lose 15 turnovers and shoot under 43 percent.

The Rockets had more energy, even though the Lakers had nearly a week to rest and plan and prepare — they were the ones who looked dead on their feet, hands on their hips as the Rockets led by as much as 19 in a slow, plodding march to a 112-97 Game 1 loss for the favored Lakers.

James compared the difficulty of preparing for their speed to lining up on the gridiron against the "Greatest Show on Turf" Rams teams: It's one thing to scout it, and another thing to line up against it.

"It's like, 'OK, we need to play them again,'" James said. "There's no way you can simulate that speed, so getting out on the floor and having a Game 1, you get a good feel for it."

The enormity of the challenge the shortest lineup in the NBA will present was apparent early, as the Lakers struggled to find the groove they hit in the last four wins against the Portland Trail Blazers in

Round 1. They couldn't find the lanes to the rim as fleet-footed Houston covered them up, and their stocky frames were able to take the pounding from the Lakers' big men.

There were shades of the Portland series Game 1, when the Lakers fell to the Blazers in a game in which their offense had all kinds of kinks with 3-pointers bouncing out and their stars looking tentative on their drives to the rim. But in losing to the Rockets, the Lakers looked a step slow on defense, too, where they failed to stop Harden (36 points, 12 for 20 shooting) and were outscored by 15 points during the 32 minutes when Westbrook was on the floor.

The Lakers pushed back on their perceived edges: They claimed that not playing in days had pulled them out a rhythm, and that not knowing who their opponent was until the final seconds of Wednesday night's Game 7 made them hedge.

"I've always felt the team that played a Game 7 has a slight advantage, but we can't look at that as any type of excuse," Lakers coach Frank Vogel said. "We're not an excuse team and we've gotta come out and compete to win a game."

The initial sequences played out like fighters cautiously circling, with neither team pulling ahead very far. It was tied at 52 late in the second quarter before the Rockets scored nine unanswered points going into the intermission, including three straight baskets from Westbrook and Harden.

The Lakers also lamented that they let Harden get to the line early: The NBA's scoring champ had 25 points by halftime.

The 35-year-old James (20 points) had moments

LeBron James drives to the basket ahead of Houston Rockets' P.J. Tucker during the first half of the 112-97 Game 1 loss. James was relatively quiet in the loss with only 20 points as the Lakers adjusted to Houston's unique style of play. (AP Images)

that seemed to turn back the clock: a second-quarter towering dunk over Westbrook cut a fearsome silhouette, and a chase down block of Westbrook in the third was capped by an end-to-end dash for his own contested finish off the glass.

But even James needs help these days. Aside from Alex Caruso (14 points), no one scored more than Danny Green's 10 points among the supporting cast. And the Lakers' mistakes hurt the most: The mistakes came on careless tosses on the perimeter and inside, as James and Rajon Rondo each had four turnovers, and Davis had three. The Rockets defense was spring-loaded and ready to run back for a total of 27 points off Lakers turnovers.

Davis led the Lakers in scoring with 25 points found some midrange rhythm on 10 for 16 shooting, but it was work: He couldn't make the cruising cuts to the rim that have been the foundation of his game this season. P.J. Tucker stationed himself like a double-wide trailer in the paint to deter him from spinning to the basket.

But ultimately beyond schematic tweaks, the Lakers felt they could have brought more energy themselves, especially on defensive possessions where they struggled to rotate as fast as the Rockets pinged the ball around the court.

"I don't think we played as hard as we could," Caruso said. "I think that falls on nobody's shoulders but our own, the five guys that are out there, and everybody else that's around them."

Even though the Lakers brought back Rondo after a lengthy absence dating to March, they were still down a man: Jason Kidd suffered what Vogel described as "severe back spasms" leaving the coaching staff down two with Lionel Hollins watching from home.

The Lakers had more fans than they've ever had in the bubble: Many of their wives and girlfriends sat a few feet back from the sideline as a handful of their children danced to pregame music. But losing is losing, and soon the Lakers' loved ones mirrored their own serious expressions.

There's a lot of series left in a best-of-seven, and the Lakers have come back before. But Game 1 served to say there are few advantages for the Lakers: They'll have to earn every inch of the way. ∎

WESTERN CONFERENCE SEMIFINALS GAME 2

SEPTEMBER 6, 2020 | LAKE BUENA VISTA, FLORIDA

LAKERS 117, ROCKETS 109

FULL SPEED

Lakers Race By Rockets as Anthony Davis, LeBron James Overpower on Offense

By Kyle Goon

In the NBA bubble, it's taken the Lakers a few extra steps to get top speed.

But once they've played their best, it's been hard for anyone to catch them.

Full speed was Sunday night, after LeBron James' clinching bucket with 32 seconds left, a fadeaway jumper, Anthony Davis met him on the other end of the court — the two Lakers stars beamed as they low-fived, confident in their eventual 117-109 triumph over the Houston Rockets to even up the series in Game 2.

Davis scored 34 points, while James was an assist shy of a triple-double with 28 points and 11 rebounds. Both outplayed the Houston Rockets' stars James Harden and Russell Westbrook, who combined for 37 points as the Lakers put on a defensive clinic, withstanding the outside assault of 22 threes from their opponent.

Like their last series, in which the Lakers revved up starting in Game 2 and beat the Blazers in four straight games, the victory was intoned with a message: The Rockets play small because they were built that way and have no other choice. But the Lakers can play any way they want — and still win.

"Be able to play big versus teams, be able to play small, be able to play in between — we built that from the beginning and we have that, always had that in our toolbox," said James, who along with Davis had a powerful say in general manager Rob Pelinka's moves last summer. "And tonight was an example of that, being able to go to that."

Frank Vogel said the plan was for the Lakers to continue to use their size: They started JaVale McGee, and Dwight Howard kept warm along the sideline. But Morris subbed in after Davis subbed out when Harden incidentally poked him in the eye, and then he made four 3-pointers in a row.

Rajon Rondo (10 points, 9 assists), the recently returned veteran point guard, knew well enough to keep feeding him, giving the Lakers a 16-point lead by the end of the first quarter. Vogel knew well enough to keep them both in.

"Sometimes you gotta ride that hot hand or the hot lineup," he said. "The plan was to play JaVale and Dwight but we obviously audibled at that point."

Playing down to Houston's size didn't change many of the Lakers' advantages: They outscored the Rockets by 28 points in the paint, and they wound up with six more rebounds after Houston battled them even on the boards in Game 1. Defensively, they held the Rockets to under 45 percent shooting, with James leading with two blocks including an emphatic volleyball swat of Westbrook in the fourth quarter.

Harden wound up with 27 points, but it was an especially rough night for Westbrook, who had 10 points on 4 for 15 shooting. He had just four assists against seven turnovers, which helped fuel the Lakers' 27 points off of Houston's 17 giveaways. Two nights

The Lakers and Rajon Rondo bounced back in Game 2, with Rondo contributing 10 points, nine assists and five steals. (AP Images)

earlier, the Rockets had scored that much themselves off of turnovers.

Finding the tables flipped, Westbrook seemed like he was searching after the loss: "Right now, I'm just runnin' around. I gotta look at film and figure out how to be effective."

Early on, the Lakers' Game 2 mojo — combined with the icy confidence in their Black Mamba jerseys — seemed to have them on the right track.

They smothered Harden and Westbrook early on with halfcourt traps and double-teams, forcing the ball out of the hands of Houston's best playmakers.

In these playoffs, there's been no more auspicious sign than Davis getting hot early: He was once again, starting out 3 for 4 from the floor and finishing his midrange looks over the head of Tucker.

In Game 1, couldn't find a way to turn around a second half slump. But on Sunday, they were prepared: The final frame saw Houston score just 17 points, with the Lakers fueled by a huge advantage in the paint and 20 fast break points.

"We're not in that situation thinking we can be down 0-2 if we lose this game," Davis said. "Our mindset is how do we win this game and we came out with a defensive mindset."

James seemed to greatly relish the closing moments of the win: His fourth quarter alley-oop from Alex Caruso stood out as one of the games' most emphatic moments. Afterward shouted to some of his friends in the burgeoning Lakers fan section.

For the Lakers, being even in their playoff series has somehow still felt like being up. After saying Friday it took time to prepare for Houston's speed, James said on Sunday that they're all caught up.

"It's something that can catch you off guard in a Game 1 situation," James said. "We got a feel for that and we understand how hard and every possession and how much scrambling and how much runnin' and how much pace and how physical the game's gonna be against this team, because they're very good, extremely good, no matter who's on the floor."

So are the Lakers. ∎

LeBron James and his teammates were more comfortable with the pace of play in Game 2, with James powering the Lakers with 28 points, 11 rebounds and nine assists. (AP Images)

KEEP THE RHYTHM

Lakers Force Their Way Past Rockets, Take Series Lead

By Kyle Goon

Afterward, they shook hands with an exhausted kind of pride.

If their win in Game 2 was emphatic, the one in Game 3 was business-like. LeBron James wiped his face wearily with a towel as the clock ran out on the Lakers' 112-102 victory on Tuesday night — his best two-way performance with the team to give the Lakers a 2-1 edge on the Houston Rockets in the Western Conference semifinals.

Perhaps as much as any game since he's been a Laker, James was at his peak. He bullied the Rockets in the lane, shoving them for space and finishing tough shots off the glass overhead. He pulled up plenty, too, hitting four of his first five 3-point attempts and leaving the Rockets to shrug as they jogged back the other way.

He finished with 36 points, 29 of them in the first half. It was enough of an effort to outpace 63 points from James Harden and Russell Westbrook, who bounced back from an underwhelming Game 2.

James was also fearsome on defense, finishing with four blocks in the third quarter alone. As the clock ran out on the third, Austin Rivers attempted to dash to the basket for a buzzer-beating lay-up — James swept in behind him like a falcon, swatting his shot off the glass and into oblivion.

James' competitiveness came out in other ways, too: He bent the ear of head referee Marc Davis play after play, arguing every bump and whistle and wholly unwilling to surrender any inch of an advantage.

It was fitting that the Lakers' sixth victory of this playoff run was also James' 162nd, passing former Laker and current Sparks coach Derek Fisher for the all-time individual lead. It was the perfect night for coach Frank Vogel to reiterate his belief that James is the most valuable player in the NBA — when likely MVP Giannis Antetokounmpo had been sidelined as his Milwaukee team was eliminated by Miami.

"We didn't play any defense in the first half, so this easily could've been a blowout if he wasn't hitting big shot after big shot, so he was spectacular with that," Vogel said. "When he's protecting the rim on that end of the floor and then scoring 30 in a half, that's just remarkable."

But the Lakers also kept pulling away during James' break in the fourth quarter thanks to defense. Houston couldn't score on five of six straight possessions, including two steals by Anthony Davis, even with Harden on the floor and James off.

The first half was a lay-up line: The Lakers allowed the Rockets to run wild on their 10 turnovers before the break, scoring 12 points. Even though they 55 percent

LeBron James was all over the court in the Game 3 win, notching 36 points, seven rebounds, five assists and four blocks. (AP Images)

for the game, they still trailed at halftime by three points with Houston capitalizing on their mistakes.

"When we went to the locker room, we watched some film, and we had conversation right away on what we could do in the second half to get better and be better," James said in his TNT interview. "And we was able to transfer that into the second half."

After fully committing to go small, yanking JaVale McGee from the starting group for the third quarter, the Lakers defense held Houston to just 38 points in the second half. Davis was bruising as the Lakers' small-ball center, scoring 26 points and grabbing a playoff-high 15 rebounds.

A surprise third star emerged too: the mythical "Playoff" Rajon Rondo, who scored 21 points and notched nine assists on 8 for 11 shooting. He nailed key 3-pointers in the closing minutes of the game.

"Playoff Rondo is real," Davis said. "And he showed up tonight."

With four-and-a-half minutes to go, the already shorthanded Rockets took another blow when Robert Covington collided with the Lakers' Davis and fell, slamming his head against the court. He went to the locker room, and Houston was forced to play the remainder of the game without him and Danuel House (who missed the game for personal reasons).

James felt a special veteran delight that he continues to set records even in his 17th season. He's never had four blocks in a quarter before Tuesday night. And while he said he isn't where he would like to be physically, owing to the unique conditions of the bubble, that playoff edge finally seems set where it usually lies throughout his historic postseason career.

"From a rhythm standpoint, I am where I would like to be and I want to continue that," he said. "It's all about playing basketball efficient, being effective out on the floor with my minutes and doing whatever it takes to help our team win. I've always been a winning player and that's all that matters to me." ■

"Playoff" Rajon Rondo showed up for Game 3, dropping 21 points and nine assists. (AP Images)

WESTERN CONFERENCE SEMIFINALS GAME 4
SEPTEMBER 10, 2020 | LAKE BUENA VISTA, FLORIDA
LAKERS 110, ROCKETS 100

CRUISE CONTROL

Lakers Send the Rockets Reeling, Take 3-1 lead in Series

By Kyle Goon

In the middle of the fourth quarter, LeBron James lined up next to the lane for a pair of Houston free throws. With a double-digit lead in hand for most of the night, James looked carefree, bouncing his hips to the strains of Aaliyah playing in the gym.

If at first you don't succeed, brush yourself off and try again.

How long ago that Game 1 loss seemed on Thursday night, when the Lakers knocked around the Houston Rockets 110-100 and took a 3-1 lead in their second-round playoff series at AdventHealth Arena.

Technically speaking, the Lakers require another win to advance. But in Game 4, the truth was laid plain: The Lakers are the better team.

It was realized by the swarming hands and quick feet of their defense, which held the Rockets' James Harden in check for almost the entire evening. It was shown in a balanced offensive effort, which allowed the Lakers to win despite just 16 points from James.

It came on a night when the Lakers fully committed to playing "small," starting Markieff Morris instead of regular center JaVale McGee to better match up with Houston's shorter, 3-point shooting group. But James pointed out that even when the Lakers go small, they're still plenty big enough to punish the Rockets — a point he emphasized by spreading his arms.

"We all have this wingspan and we play hard," James said. "When you have that type of length, when you have that type of athleticism, throughout five guys, it definitely helps clean the glass. Defend. Be

able to rotate. Be able to be in communication, where if something breaks down, you have guys that can fly around and help as well. It's a good lineup for us."

The Lakers walloped the Rockets for most of the game, their switchable scheme and timely double-teams mostly keeping Harden off the ball. He scored just 21 points, the fewest he's gotten in this series, and the Rockets managed just 41 points in the first half as a result. The Lakers led by as much as 23 points, rotating with breezy confidence, their defense seemingly ironclad.

Then the Rockets came out of hibernation late in the fourth quarter. Russell Westbrook led a 22-4 charge that nearly caught the Lakers in their victory lap. The last of Harden's 20 free throw attempts closed the gap to just five points with 58 seconds left.

But even then, the Lakers had an answer, closing with a 3-pointer from Alex Caruso (16 points) and an emphatic jam from James, all but shutting the book on Houston in the game and in the series that has left them looking out of steam and out of the ability to change their approach.

"I didn't have one second guess if I was gonna hit him in that corner when I seen that he had a little bit of space," James said of Caruso. "And he knows that I have the confidence in him to knock it down."

Though Anthony Davis finished with a game-high 29 points, it was a night where the team's depth shined on the offensive end as James and Davis were targeted by Rockets' double-teams. Six Lakers scored in double figures, and everyone who played scored — even

Anthony Davis smothers Houston's James Harden, part of an impressive defensive effort by the Lakers limiting Harden to only 21 points on 2 for 11 shooting. (AP Images)

rookie Talen Horton-Tucker.

Though the Lakers played without two of their best rebounders in McGee and Dwight Howard, their superior length still gave them massive advantages on the glass (52 to 26), paint scoring (62 to 24) and second-chance points (17 to 3). Davis had 12 rebounds, but James led the team with 15, just an assist shy of a triple double.

But the lineup change also allowed the Lakers to more effectively chase the Rockets off the 3-point line: For the second straight game, a team that averaged a league-high 45 threes per game shot 33 or fewer, forcing them inside the arc where they have to deal with the shot-blocking prowess of Davis and James.

"When you have the confidence you can go 4-5-6 possessions where you're just squeezing the other team's offense," Coach Frank Vogel said, "getting stops and then with our ability to run the floor with LeBron James being the quarterback of that action and being in attack mode, we have strong belief in what we can accomplish as a group."

The series has seen the Lakers sharpening their claws: Their double-teams and schemes to chase 3-point shooters off the line has become more precise, and on offense, they've become less reliant on superhuman scoring nights from James and Davis.

It wouldn't matter much if the Rockets had answers to the Lakers' strategies, because they don't have the manpower. Danuel House missed a second straight game after it was revealed in media reports that he was under investigation for a violation of bubble protocols.

With the Clippers up 3-1 in their series against the Denver Nuggets, a possible first-ever All-L.A. series seems on the horizon in the Western Conference Finals. And for the Lakers, the growth they've shown in this series has lit the pathway to how far they can go.

"We can play big, we can play small, we can play in between and we have the lineup to do so," said Davis. "But the players have confidence in each other, the coaches have confidence in the players which makes our team special." ∎

WESTERN CONFERENCE SEMIFINALS GAME 5

SEPTEMBER 12, 2020 | LAKE BUENA VISTA, FLORIDA

LAKERS 119, ROCKETS 96

NO MERCY

Lakers Crush Rockets to Advance to the Western Conference Finals

By Kyle Goon

As early as the first quarter, LeBron James emanated a meanness that he holds in reserve for these moments. Closeout games, he's said, are the hardest games to win. But as he knocked down one of his three 3-pointers Saturday evening to give his team a then-16 point lead just six minutes in, he sneered as he stalked back to the bench.

There would be no comeback Saturday night. Not against the Lakers, who not only outplayed Houston in a 119-96 win in Game 5 to advance to the Western Conference Finals but played their own smallball style in superior fashion.

By the fourth quarter, they were crushing Houston by as much as 30 points, watching the spirit leak out of their fourth-seeded opponent.

Six Lakers total scored in double figures, but James was at the heart of it, scoring 29 points with 11 rebounds and 7 assists. His persona was the ruthless competitor who now has a 37-10 record in closeout games.

It was the LeBron that was Promised, the one Lakers fans hoped for back when he signed in 2018. And it's the one that has helped guide the franchise back toward a championship trajectory after an unprecedented dry spell.

"I know what my name comes with, and it comes with winning," he said. "I take that responsibility to the utmost than anything. Because I am a winner and I've always been a winner."

As the Lakers spent the closing minutes cheering on the end of their bench, Houston's stars James Harden and Russell Westbrook sat with thousand-yard stares. Harden had 30 points, but Westbrook had just 10.

Going to the Western Conference Finals marks a return to glory a decade in the making for the Lakers, whose 16th championship came in 2010 when they last reached (and surpassed) that round. As ever, Lakers seasons are measured in championships, and quickly the team's attention will shift ahead to the winner the other Western second-round series which could conclude as soon as Sunday afternoon with the Clippers poised for a second attempt at their own closeout over the Nuggets.

James is no stranger to these late stages of the season, but for Anthony Davis, it was the furthest he's ever been. The Lakers' prize summer addition looked uneven on offense with 13 points and 6 turnovers, but made up for it with defensive effort, including 11 rebounds as the Lakers earned a 50-31 edge.

"I just feel like everything is falling in place," Davis said. "When I got here, obviously the goal is to win a

Anthony Davis had a relatively quiet game with only 13 points and 11 rebounds, but still helped propel the Lakers to the Western Conference Finals for the first time since 2010. (AP Images)

championship and we're eight wins away."

Perhaps because the Lakers expected so much desperation from the Rockets, they came out with an extra dose of pep: With James charging and their 3-point shooters firing, they quickly shot up the scoreboard to a 13-2 lead. Houston called a panicked timeout minutes in as James emphatically dunked, sending a restless Lakers bench exploding onto the court in early celebration.

But Harden, who had been cowed into just two made field goals in Game 4, was lively early and had 19 points by halftime. Davis struggled to find a rhythm, scoring his first basket at the 2:46 mark of the second quarter. Though the Lakers never trailed, they looked frustrated headed into halftime with an 11-point lead, both with calls and the 13 team turnovers.

But a smothering third quarter, in which the Lakers only allowed 18 points, did the Rockets in. It was the only time Houston had been held under 100 points in the playoffs.

The Lakers outdid the Rockets at their own 3-point shooting prowess, hitting 19 for 37 from deep including four 3-pointers apiece from Markieff Morris (16 points) and Danny Green (14 points). Kyle Kuzma rounded out the scoring effort with 17 points from the bench.

The Rockets went out kicking and screaming — literally in the case of Russell Westbrook, who got into a fourth-quarter shouting match with William Rondo, Rajon Rondo's brother, who ESPN reported was waving "goodbye" as the Lakers' lead ballooned past 20 points. Westbrook had to be restrained by an official as William Rondo was asked by security to leave the arena. The NBA has fan conduct rules for player guests read before every game.

Rondo told The Undefeated that his brother simply called Westbrook "trash." Westbrook, known for his tempestuous demeanor, had a different account.

"When you cross that line then he supposed to be at home, there's no rules or regulations for that," he said.

"But he started talking crazy but I don't play that game."

But Westbrook and Houston's problems are just beginning following elimination. It seemed to bring an end to a once-promising era for the franchise, which made four second-round appearances under coach Mike D'Antoni, whose contract is up after this season. After committing fully to their micro-sized roster, the Rockets have troubling offseason issues, which also including more than $80 million committed to two stars who have not brought them to the Finals.

These things were likely hanging on the mind of Houston general manager Daryl Morey, who back in October sent a Lakers' trip to China into a tailspin over a tweet. But he carried an air of grace as he walked back near the Lakers' locker room afterward to shake the hand of rival GM Rob Pelinka and wish him well in the next round.

Frank Vogel lavished praise on his defense, which has now quieted an impressive cadre of scorers, including Portland's Damian Lillard and C.J. McCollum in addition to Harden and Westbrook. After another Game 1 disappointment, the Lakers have convincingly adjusted to look much like the strongest contender remaining in the championship field based on their playoff body of work.

But the goal is not to be the strongest in the middle: It's to be the strongest at the end. And James is ready for that chase next.

"It's the reason I wanted to be a part of this franchise: To take 'em back to a place they were accustomed to being," he said in his walk-off interview. "And that's competing for a championship." ∎

James Harden bounced back in Game 5 with 30 points but only 11 of those came in the second half, as the Lakers turned up the defense and sent the Rockets home from the bubble. (AP Images)

WESTERN CONFERENCE FINALS GAME 1

SEPTEMBER 18, 2020 | LAKE BUENA VISTA, FLORIDA

LAKERS 126, NUGGETS 114

OUT OF THE STARTING BLOCKS

Lakers Start Strong This Time, Blow Out Nuggets in Game 1

By Kyle Goon

There was one thing that Denver didn't want the Western Conference Finals to be: a track meet.

That's exactly the kind of series the Lakers had in mind.

Sprints, like the long loping strides to the basket that led to 16 fast break points and 20 points off turnovers. High jumps, like the ones Anthony Davis, Dwight Howard and LeBron James used to slam down lobs for much of the night. Shotput, or something like it, as James and Rajon Rondo heaved passes downstream on the way to a team total 33 assists.

The Nuggets have been the underdog of the NBA bubble with their 3-1 comebacks, but the Lakers are No. 1 for a reason. Behind Davis' 37 points and 10 rebounds, the Lakers got out to a good start of playing the favorite in a 126-114 blowout of Denver, which will have to come back again to survive.

"We want to be the most physical team on the floor every time we take the floor, regardless of who we're playing," Lakers coach Frank Vogel said. "And we have a physical team. We've got big, strong guys. But a lot of times teams with big, strong guys don't have the speed to match it, and we have the ability to do both."

Davis' aggression was most pronounced in the third, when he scored 16 of his points thriving in the Lakers' uptempo style that Denver coach Mike Malone had said just the day before he wished to avoid.

Davis' All-NBA counterpart Nikola Jokic (21 points) had a few bright moments, but was unable to string together much momentum with foul trouble. Jamal Murray, a lights-out shooter in so many tight games this postseason, was held to 21.

While the Nuggets were able to bottle up James' scoring (15 points, all in the first half), he was content to pick apart the defense with 12 assists. It seemed possible that James, who had finished a distant second-place to MVP finisher Giannis Antetokounmpo earlier in the day, was motivated by the perceived sleight: 16 out of 101 first-place votes.

Earlier Vogel told the press that a championship mattered most to James, who has won four MVP awards to his three rings. But it seems MVP matters to him, too.

"I never came to this league saying, 'Be MVP or be a champion,'" he said. "I've always said I just want to get better and better every single day and those things will take care of itself, but some things is just out of my hand and some things you can't control but, it pisses me off."

It was a night for the old heads on the team: After a turbulent first quarter of trying to contain Jokic, the Lakers subbed in the 34-year-old Howard, who immediately shoved Jokic and proceeded to play a physical game against Denver's size. After playing just five minutes in the previous series against Houston,

Dwight Howard throws down two of his 13 points as the Lakers took Game 1 over the Nuggets in commanding fashion. (AP Images)

Howard burst with energy in a 13-point, two-block and two-steal performance.

Just two days before, he had acknowledged that isolation inside the bubble without the outlet of playing time had been difficult. Howard didn't want to miss his chance to enforce some of his will on Jokic.

"As soon as I step onto the court, I'm gonna let him know that I'm there," he said. "We're staying at same hotel, I might meet him right outside his room, let him know for the rest of the series, I'm gonna be right here, locked onto you. It's not nothing bad, it's just the competitive spirit inside of me."

Rondo had nine assists, putting him at 10th all-time ahead of Michael Jordan in postseason dimes. Perhaps most notably, he contributed zero turnovers on the night. As a team, the Lakers had 33 assists on 44 baskets, with just 11 turnovers.

After losing Game 1 in their previous two series to Portland and Houston and with another six-day layoff from game action, the Lakers made a point to come out swinging Friday. Both the Lakers and the Nuggets were active early, scoring a combined 74 points in the first quarter.

The initial promise of a shootout slowly slid into a free throw shooting contest as the Lakers drew whistle after whistle. In the second quarter alone, the Lakers took 24 free throws (and made only 14). Jokic and Jamal Murray fell prey to the fouls themselves, both getting three apiece by the early third quarter.

By the third quarter, the scoreboard indicated that the Lakers didn't have much to fear as they held on to a double-digit margin. But given Denver's penchant for comebacks, the Lakers didn't want to let up.

"No lead is safe with this team," Davis said. "Not in a game, not in a series."

In Game 1, the Lakers didn't relent. They'll need three more efforts just like it — a challenge no one has yet met against the Nuggets. ■

Denver Nuggets' Michael Porter Jr. and Los Angeles Lakers' Alex Caruso compete for control of a loose ball during the second half of the series-opening win for Los Angeles. (AP Images)

WESTERN CONFERENCE FINALS GAME 2

SEPTEMBER 20, 2020 | LAKE BUENA VISTA, FLORIDA

LAKERS 105, NUGGETS 103

HOLLYWOOD ENDING

On Stunning Anthony Davis Game-Winner, Lakers Top Nuggets in Game 2

By Kyle Goon

The biggest shot of Anthony Davis' career was a career in the making.

It took game-winning misses — the one in Brooklyn in March from very nearly the exact same spot — that kept Davis in a rut for four days afterward, promising he would bury it next time. It took memories of Kobe Bryant, the king of the big shot, and the Black Mamba jersey that clung to his chest to honor the Lakers legend. It took hours of practices, working on end-of-game plays to the point where not a word or a timeout was needed to run it precisely as designed.

Sometimes all the threads cinch together at once. And that was how, at the moment he let a buzzer-beating 3-point fadeaway over the outstretched arm of Nikola Jokic, that Davis knew — just knew — that it would strike true.

No one knows more than Davis, who positioned himself last year to be traded to the Lakers, how much weight that shot carried.

"When I left, I just wanted to be able to compete for a championship," he said, "and I know that moments like this comes with it."

It was a moment: a stunning game-winner from the left wing to give the Lakers a 105-103 win in Game 2 of the Western Conference Finals over the Denver Nuggets — a game they would have rightly deserved to lose if Davis hadn't saved them. But he did, capping a 31-point night in brilliant fashion, going stride-for-stride not just against Jokic, his All-NBA counterpart, but the extravagant expectations that have followed him ever since June, when he landed on this team via a blockbuster trade.

The Lakers took a 2-0 lead in devastating fashion. As Denver coach Michael Malone said later: "No silver linings."

The game itself made the Lakers look mortal: After building a 10-point halftime lead, they wilted in the second, looking all out of sorts in their half court sets. The last possession was largely an extension of those struggles, as Alex Caruso missed an open look from the top of the arc, then Danny Green's quick follow up on an offensive rebound was rejected out of bounds by Jamal Murray (25 points).

But with two seconds left without a timeout, the Lakers did a number of things seamlessly: Rajon Rondo checked in for Caruso to make the inbounds pass, approaching coach Frank Vogel on his own accord: "He knew the play; he saw what formation we were in," Vogel explained. From his baseline perch, Rondo took in what wasn't available: a backdoor cut, or a lob over the top of Jokic, who was guarding the pass. James didn't move from his spot in the elbow, but Davis, anticipating an open deep look, cut over top to the 3-point line while his defender Mason

Anthony Davis (3) watches his last-second, game-winning 3-point shot fly, a devastating blow to the Nuggets as the Lakers took a 2-0 series lead. (AP Images)

Plumlee dropped inexplicably into the paint.

It was an easy bounce pass for Rondo and a not-so-easy shot for Davis, even if he made it look effortless. Afterward during a press conference in the attached practice gym, James pointed to the court beneath him and described all the scenarios that the Lakers had practiced and drilled into their heads, trying to account for every possible scenario.

"You want to be a championship club," James said, "you have to be able to do that on the fly."

The game-winner swept aside all manner of playoff sins: The Lakers had surrendered a 16-point lead against the team that has been least kind to front-runners in the playoffs. They gave up 24 turnovers in the game, which was the most a winning team had surrendered in the playoffs in two seasons. Before Davis took the final attempt, the Lakers were just 7 for 20 from the field.

Those miscues allowed the Nuggets to crawl back, as did the relentless second-half effort of Jokic, who scored 12 of his 30 points in the fourth quarter. The final three baskets positioned the 7-foot Serbian to play hero himself: a 3-pointer with a minute left, a go-ahead tip-in, and a hook shot that he made space for by backing down Davis all the way into the paint.

On that last one, Denver led by a point with 20 seconds left, which pushed the Lakers to use their final timeout — another comeback story for the Never-Die Nuggets.

"Leads mean nothing against this team," Vogel said. "They are a nightmare to guard."

Davis took the last basket personally, thinking that he could have defended Jokic better. Rondo told him to not worry about it: "Now go get it back."

To that point, Davis had traded buckets with Jokic. While James started out the hottest for the Lakers, notching his team's first 12 points while his teammates went 0 for 12 in to start the game, Davis had caught on later, and scored 22 of his points in the second half.

A 3-pointer with three minutes to go portended his later success, giving the Lakers an eight-point lead, but they couldn't hold it. The only reason they were within a point at the end is because Davis scored a floater over Jokic with 26 seconds left.

After his final shot, Davis dashed toward the Lakers bench rushing back at him, and screamed: "KO-BE." The Lakers improved to 3-0 in these playoffs while wearing their Black Mamba uniforms, a detail Vogel pointed out in the team huddle.

"Every time we put on those jerseys, obviously we're representing him," Davis said. "Especially in those jerseys, it's his jersey, one he created, and any time we put it on we want to win."

It was the kind of shot, and the kind of game, that builds one's reputation as a winner. In the NBA, the 27-year-old Davis has never won this big. But LeBron James (26 points), his teammate and mentor who has won titles, saw a blossom of growth in the young star which he acknowledged afterward: "That's why I wanted him here so badly."

For James, there was a parallel: He once hit a game-winner against the Orlando Magic in Game 2 of the Eastern Conference Finals in 2009 (against his now-teammate Dwight Howard). It was one of his favorite moments of his career at that time, James said, and he wished that Davis could have been enveloped by the adoration of Staples Center — "it probably would have blew the roof off."

But it wasn't about the fans who weren't there, or the gleeful reception of J.R. Smith and a bowled-over Talen Horton-Tucker who were, James said. In his view, it was about Davis, calmly stroking the shot, then posing imperiously afterward with balled fists, showing the competitor and winner it's taken him years to become.

"It's just the confidence to take the shot," James said. "You're not going to make them all, but the belief to just take it and live with the results is what it's all about. Tonight was his moment." ■

Anthony Davis celebrates with his teammates following the dramatic win, which also gave the superstar Davis the first big-stage signature moment of his career. (AP Images)

WESTERN CONFERENCE FINALS GAME 3

SEPTEMBER 22, 2020 | LAKE BUENA VISTA, FLORIDA

NUGGETS 114, LAKERS 106

NO MATCH FOR DESPERATION

Lakers Make a Late Charge But Can't Catch Nuggets in Game 3

By Kyle Goon

For a spellbinding eight minutes, the Lakers were poised for their own Nuggets moment.

Playing out of a zone defense, the breaker of high school attacks that has curiously had a similar effect on NBA teams in the bubble, the bull rush of their transition offense powered by LeBron James and Anthony Davis seemed hell-bent on completely erasing a Denver lead. It took only nine possessions to cut a 20-point margin to 3, in a game that had the power to put the Western Conference Finals fully under the Lakers' control.

It was almost good enough — but the Lakers used their best punches far too late.

The Nuggets held on in the final minutes to win 114-106 on Tuesday thanks to a pair of late threes by Jamal Murray (28 points) that sandwiched a lay-up by Paul Millsap, putting them on the board in the series, which the Lakers lead 2-1.

The finish was undermined by the middle, when the Lakers' lack of urgency cost them on the glass (44-25 Denver advantage), on defense (the Nuggets shot 56 percent in the first three quarters) and in turnovers (16, leading to 25 points). It has breathed life into the Nuggets, who have been notorious for knocking out complacent front-runners. For the first time, the reality settled in that the Lakers could be the next favorite to fall if they don't change course.

"When you dig yourself a hole like that, every shot that they make and every shot that we miss, feels like the game is collapsing," said James, who scored 30 points including 13 in the fourth. "So you know, we played some pretty good ball in the fourth quarter, but those first 36 minutes, that hurt us obviously."

There was still 10:36 left in the fourth quarter when Murray broke into the lane against a shoddy Lakers defense and threw down a one-handed jam. The bearded scoring phenom roared with the defiance that has defined his Denver team's playoff campaign, while the Lakers peered up at the scoreboard to squint at a 20-point deficit.

Two off-target 3-point attempts by the Lakers in the final minutes could have tied it, from Kentavious Caldwell-Pope and then James. Davis (27 points) lamented a transition miscommunication between he and Rajon Rondo (8 assists) that should have been a "guaranteed two points."

The Lakers finished with 20 fastbreak points and 21 points off of turnovers, outscoring their challengers 31-21 in the final frame.

"We were right there, we're down three, 98-101. Kenny comes in, wide-open look: We all thought it was good," Davis said. "If he makes that, it's a tie game and anything happens."

But Denver's energy and coordination were insurmountable for the Lakers, who lacked both of those things for long stretches on Tuesday night.

The Game 3 switch to Denver's "home court" prompted Coach Frank Vogel to joke about having to "always account for altitude." But even if it wasn't the

Jamal Murray and the Nuggets got back into the series with a 114-96 Game 3 win, as the Denver guard went off for 28 points. (AP Images)

elevation, something had the Lakers running at half-speed against the Nuggets, who seemed inspired after taking a tough Game 2 loss by a Davis buzzer-beater.

The Lakers' small lineup that had worked wonders against the Houston Rockets was completely run over by the Monte Morris- and Michael Porter Jr.-led bench. A 15-2 run to start the second quarter set the dynamic for the rest of the game, where for once the Lakers were the pursuers.

Jerami Grant far outshone any of the Lakers' role players with 26 points in 33 minutes, on a night when star Denver big Nikola Jokic was held to 22 points and coughed up five turnovers. No Lakers player outside of Davis and James had more than Caldwell-Pope's 12.

While the Lakers have attempted to drill into their minds that their foes — the authors of two unlikely series comebacks — should be feared, they've struggled to match the desperation of Denver. Before the blistering Game 3 fourth-quarter finish, the Nuggets had outscored the Lakers in five straight quarters of the series.

Davis (27 points) insisted afterward that the Lakers still have control. But without his own Game 2 winner, the Lakers are aware that they would be staring down a very different series where they have often not played like the more talented team. He acknowledged his own total of two rebounds showed how much more he could give.

"It's unacceptable," he said. "There's not really much I can say. I just have to be better." ■

WESTERN CONFERENCE FINALS GAME 4

SEPTEMBER 24, 2020 | LAKE BUENA VISTA, FLORIDA

LAKERS 114, NUGGETS 108

BROWBEATING

LeBron James and Anthony Davis Combined for 60 points to Take 3-1 Lead

By Kyle Goon

Either the Lakers are poised to do what no team has done yet in these playoffs, or the Denver Nuggets are positioned right where they want to be.

After a Game 4 dogfight Thursday, which saw Anthony Davis and LeBron James wrestle for 60 combined points and hold off an awe-inspiring assault from Jamal Murray, the Lakers won 114-108 and now hold a 3-1 lead in the Western Conference Finals. It's proven to be the most difficult series lead to hold against these Nuggets who have come back from that deficit twice already.

The Lakers have been confident closers themselves, already banishing the Portland Trail Blazers and Houston Rockets in their first closeout opportunities. But Davis said it would be foolhardy to think, especially after a tight Game 4, that Denver is close to feeling beat.

"You can never be comfortable around this team … this team is not going to go away," Davis said. "We gotta put 'em away."

The Lakers were able to win thanks much in part to their stars' aggression. Davis (34 points) was 10 for 15 from the field, while James (26 points) was 7 for 18. The game-changer was their ability to get to the free throw line, which accounted for 24 of their points. They combined for 13 of those free throws in the fourth quarter alone, and James (who is not a strong free throw shooter) was 7 for 8 in the final period.

The Lakers outshot the Nuggets at the foul line by 11 in the game, and they made more (28) than Denver attempted (23).

Murray was sensational, despite not hitting a 3-point shot. He went 12 for 20 from the field, including a wide variety of lay-ups, floaters and sudden-stop jumpers. He also added eight assists.

James was pivotal in two late stops on Murray near the rim. While Denver called for fouls on both lay-up attempts, the Lakers were able to manufacture points out of the ensuing possessions. James also made a pair of free throws in the final minute giving the Lakers a seven-point lead.

It was the fourth quarter when James asked for the assignment. Frank Vogel let him have at it, and while Murray made two assists and four free throws in the last six minutes, he did not make a field goal during that stretch.

"I know it's winning time and Jamal had it going: Kid is special," James said. "I told my teammates that I had him and everyone else could kind of stay at bay and stay home."

The Lakers looked for a major shake-up after Game 3 when they were lackluster on defense and on the glass for the first three quarters. Dwight Howard, who

Anthony Davis challenges Denver's Mason Plumlee at the rim in the first half of the Game 4 win. Davis led the Lakers in scoring with 34 points on 12 for 15 shooting. (AP Images)

made his first start of the playoffs, fit both bills and made an impact early, getting 8 points and 8 rebounds (four on the offensive glass) by the end of his first stint.

Howard finished with 12 points and 11 rebounds in his 22 minutes. The Lakers outrebounded Denver by eight, a major shortcoming in the previous game. Nikola Jokic had 16 points and just seven rebounds, and also struggled with foul trouble.

Frank Vogel said he wanted to set a tone by bringing Howard, a three-time Defensive Player of the Year early in his career, in to start.

"We lost Game 3, and in the loss, his energy was, to me, infectious," Vogel said. "We knew what he could do in this matchup."

It helped that Davis was absolutely unstoppable on offense, making his first seven field goal attempts, as well as first five free throws, before finally missing a shot in 20 minutes into the game.

Murray, however, was willing to meet him nearly shot for shot. Among his first-half highlights was an impossible lay-up that saw him switch hands midair and scoop from under off the glass — mimicking a famous Michael Jordan highlight almost exactly.

Though the Lakers led by as much as 12 in the first half, they only had a five-point lead at the intermission, and the game largely was a single-digit affair after that.

There was one scare midway through the second half as Davis turned his left ankle, and grabbed at it on the ground grimacing. Moments later, he was able to walk off the pain and play through while hitting free throws on a foul call.

James joked that the Lakers gauge his level of focus by how low he sets his trademark unibrow on off days.

"Yesterday, his brow was very low … and no one talked to him," James said. "So we already knew the mindset that he was in. He came out and did it." ∎

LeBron James played his typical all-around dominant game, with 26 points, nine rebounds and eight assists. (AP Images)

WESTERN CONFERENCE FINALS GAME 5

SEPTEMBER 26, 2020 | LAKE BUENA VISTA, FLORIDA

LAKERS 117, NUGGETS 107

TRIUMPHANT RETURN

LeBron James, Lakers Punch Out Nuggets in Game 5, Advance to NBA Finals

By Kyle Goon

The Lakers have always — one way or another — found a way to float to the NBA's biggest stage.

A decade was long enough to wait. LeBron James made sure it wouldn't be any longer.

After a jaunt through NBA history, the Denver Nuggets met the one thing they could not overcome: The 35-year-old James in a closeout opportunity, smelling a path to his ninth Finals in 10 years. The star of his era rose to the moment of Game 5, nailing four straight shots in the final four minutes to seal an unforgettable cap to a masterful Game 5 victory, 117-107, that saw him score 38 points, grab 16 rebounds and dish out 10 assists.

LeBron James is going to the Finals, and the Lakers are going with him.

He choked out the last fight from Denver, which had won six straight elimination games headed into Saturday night. And even as he sat on the court in a near-empty AdventHealth Arena, he started looking ahead. There's four more wins left to a championship, and if James' will a closeout game was any indication, he's impatient to finish the whole thing.

"I do not want to play another game: That's always been my mindset," he said. "I want to be just as desperate as my opponent."

The clinching nine-point run was the stuff legendary runs are made of: James hit a stepback, a turnaround fadeaway, a pullup and a 3-pointer in one two-minute sequence to put the Nuggets to bed as the Lakers won the Western Conference Finals, 4-1. It's the first time the Lakers have been to the Finals in 10 years, the longest drought in franchise history.

"My shoulders is wide enough to carry a lot of load," James said in his postgame walkoff interview, posing next to his first-ever Western Conference trophy he's earned on his way to 10 career Finals.

Said Anthony Davis: "He told us it was his time."

To reach the Finals, the Lakers had to survive one of the Nuggets' famous comebacks. They seemed ready to pile on the Nuggets in the third quarter and led by as much as 16, then Nikola Jokic — hamstrung with foul trouble all night — picked up his fourth foul.

Moments later, a hard shoulder to the chin by Howard sent Paul Millsap sprawling to the floor, and the veteran forward sprung up ready for a scrap. Millsap had sparked an exchange with Marcus Morris in the second round against the Clippers in a Game 5 when the Nuggets were down by 16 — and this foul had a similar effect.

The Nuggets clawed their way back to even, but a late shot by Davis (27 points) from the perimeter gave the Lakers a 3-point lead headed into the fourth quarter.

Anthony Davis and the Lakers ran through Nikola Jokic and the Nuggets on their way to clinching the franchise's 31st appearance in the NBA Finals. (AP Images)

The Lakers are now 53-0 this season when leading into the final frame. James imbues this Lakers team with a closing confidence.

"When you got two great captains and great player leadership like we have with Anthony and LeBron, who are super focused and have the ability on the floor to dominate long stretches of games, you have a chance," Frank Vogel said. "So I just feel like this game, tonight, we knew what this team was capable of with their survival instincts and I was just proud of how locked in we were."

Jokic and Murray were held to just 39 combined points, their lowest mutual output of the series.

The Lakers have been to the Finals 31 times in their history, winning 16 titles. A 17th championship would tie them for most in NBA history with their league rival the Boston Celtics — who are fighting back from a 3-2 deficit to the Miami Heat in the Eastern Conference Finals and face another elimination game on Sunday.

James is attempting to become a member of an exclusive club: If the Lakers win the Finals, he would become one of four men to win championships with three different teams, joining Robert Horry and John Salley (Lakers guard Danny Green would become the other new member). But no one has ever done it as the franchise player in three places, and given that James is 35 and the NBA's career leader in playoff wins, minutes and points, it's an achievement that would stand alone in NBA history.

James improved his own immaculate closeout record with 3-1 leads, improving to 15-0 in such games. His triple-double was his 27th in his playoff career, just three shy of one Magic Johnson.

With the unusual stretch of the calendar year, something happened that never has before: The Lakers won on Jeanie Buss' birthday. Several staffers sent the Lakers' team governor messages that they would win

Game 5 for her. It's the first time the Lakers have been to the Finals in 10 years, a decade that saw the death of her father, Dr. Jerry Buss, as well as Kobe Bryant, who guided the Lakers to the promised land the last time in 2010.

That series was decided in seven games, a hard-fought rock fight with Boston. At the time, it was hard to imagine that the climb back to the NBA's biggest stage would be a lot harder than the fight that earned them that last trophy.

James took a moment to appreciate another echo with Bryant, who played a pivotal fourth quarter back in 2010 to win a closeout game against the Phoenix Suns with the same sense of confidence James had against the Nuggets.

"I'm one of the few that can understand the mindset that he played with, and the journey from high school to the NBA," he said. "So that's just a thing that I carry with me."

The wait for the Finals itself will end within a week, either Wednesday if Miami wins Game 6, or Friday if the ECF goes seven games.

The Lakers donned special hats and shirts afterward, and dapped each other up in a celebratory locker room. James teased Davis as the clock ticked near 1 a.m. in Florida, telling him he wanted to make last call at Three Bridges, the restaurant in the bubble. But it was not a final sense of cheer for the Lakers.

As Markieff Morris walked out of the building, he shouted toward the press while holding four fingers in the air: "Fo' more!" ∎

The Lakers celebrate after beating the Nuggets in Game 5 and advancing to the Finals, where they would pursue the 17th championship in franchise history. (AP Images)

SOUTHERN CALIFORNIA NEWS GROUP

Los Angeles Daily News
dailynews.com

THE ORANGE COUNTY REGISTER
ocregister.com

PRESS-TELEGRAM
presstelegram.com

DAILY BREEZE
dailybreeze.com

THE PRESS-ENTERPRISE
pe.com

Pasadena Star-News
pasadenastarnews.com

INLAND VALLEY DAILY BULLETIN
dailybulletin.com

THE SUN
sbsun.com

Redlands Daily Facts
redlandsdailyfacts.com

SAN GABRIEL VALLEY TRIBUNE
sgvtribune.com

Whittier Daily News
whittierdailynews.com

MediaNews Group

Local Brand Leaders — Known and Trusted for Over 100 Years

As premium local content providers, each of the SCNG newspapers has a long history of editorial excellence in their own respective markets — forming a special kind of trust and brand loyalty that readers really value. Exclusive local content sets the Southern California News Group apart, providing readers and users with news and information they won't find anywhere else. From local elections to their home team's top scores, when area residents need late-breaking news, SCNG newspapers, websites and mobile media are their number one resource.